THE UNITED STATES AND CHILE

Other Titles in the Contemporary Inter-American Relations Series
edited by Jorge Domínguez and Rafael Fernández de Castro

The United States and Mexico: Between Partnership and Conflict
Jorge Domínguez and Rafael Fernández de Castro

The United States and Chile: Coming in from the Cold
David R. Mares and Francisco Rojas Aravena

The United States and Venezuela: Rethinking a Relationship
Janet Kelly and Carlos A. Romero

The United States and Argentina: Changing Relations in a Changing World
Deborah Norden and Roberto Russell

CONTEMPORARY INTER-AMERICAN RELATIONS

THE UNITED STATES AND CHILE

COMING IN FROM THE COLD

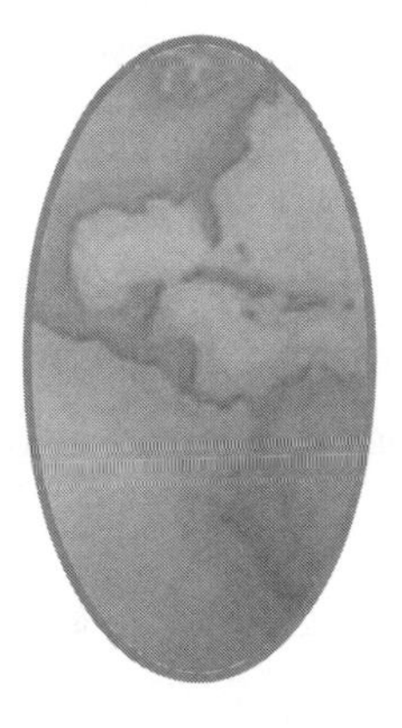

DAVID R. MARES
AND FRANCISCO ROJAS ARAVENA

ROUTLEDGE
New York London

Published in 2001 by
Routledge
29 West 35th Street
New York, New York 10001

Published in Great Britain by
Routledge
11 New Fetter Lane
London EC4P 4EE

Routledge is an imprint of the Taylor & Francis Group.

Printed in the United States of America on acid-free paper.

10 9 8 7 6 5 4 3 2 1

Library of Congress Cataloging-in-Publication Data

Mares, David R.
The Unted States and Chile: coming in from the cold / David R. Mares and Francisco Rojas Aravena.
p. cm. — (Contemporary inter-American relations)
Includes bibliographical references and index.
ISBN 0-415-93124-X (hb) — ISBN 0-415-93125-8 (pb)
1. United States—Foreign relations—Chile. 2. Chile—Foreign relations—United States. I. Rojas Aravena, Francisco. II. Title. III. Series.

JZ1480.A57 C5 2001
327.73083—dc21

2001016596

CONTENTS

SERIES PREFACE

The transition from authoritarian rule to constitutional government.

The continentwide economic depression of the 1980s and the subsequent shift toward more open market–conforming economies.

The end of the Cold War in Europe.

The transformation of relations with the United States.

EACH OF THESE MAJOR EVENTS AND PROCESSES WAS AN epochal change in the history of Latin America and the Caribbean. More striking is that all four changes took place within the same relatively short period, though not all four affected each and every country in the same way. They became interconnected, with change in each dimension fostering convergent changes in other dimensions. Thus at the beginning of the new millennium we witnessed an important transformation and intensification in U.S.–Latin American relations.

This book is part of a series of ten books on U.S. relations with Latin American and Caribbean countries. Each of these books is focused on the fourth of these four transformations, namely, the change in U.S. relations with Latin America and the Caribbean. Our premise is that the first three transformations provide pieces of the explanation for the change in U.S. relations with its neighbors in the Americas and for the changes in the foreign policies of Latin American and Caribbean states. Each of the books in the series assesses the impact of the epoch-making changes upon each other.

The process of widest impact was the economic transformation. By the end of 1982, much of North America, western Europe, and East Asia was launching into an economic boom at the very instant when Latin America was plunging into an economic depression of great severity that lasted approximately to the end of the decade. As a consequence of such economic collapse, nearly all Latin American governments readjusted their economic strategies. They departed from principal reliance on import-substitution industrialization, opened their economies to international trade and investment, and adopted policies to create more open market–conforming economies. (Even Cuba had changed its economic strategy by the 1990s, making its economy more open to foreign direct investment and trade.)

The regionwide economic changes had direct and immediate impact upon U.S.–Latin American relations. The share of U.S. trade accounted for by Latin America and the Caribbean had declined fairly steadily from the end of World War II to the end of the 1980s. In the 1990s, in contrast, U.S. trade with Latin America grew at a rate significantly faster than the growth of U.S. trade worldwide; Latin America had become the fastest-growing market for U.S. exports. The United States, at long last, took notice of Latin America. Trade between some Latin American countries also boomed, especially within subregions such as the southern cone of South America, Venezuela and Colombia, the Central American countries, and, to a lesser extent, the Anglophone Caribbean countries. The establishment of formal freer-trade areas facilitated the growth of trade and other economic relations. These included the North American Free Trade Agreement (NAFTA), which grouped Mexico, the United States, and Canada; the Mercosur (southern common market), with Argentina, Brazil, Paraguay, and Uruguay; the Andean Community, whose members were Bolivia, Colombia, Ecuador, Peru, and Venezuela; the Central American Common Market (CACM); and the Caribbean Community (CARICOM). U.S. foreign direct and portfolio investments flowed into Latin America and the Caribbean in large quantities, financing the expansion of tradable economic activities; the speed of portfolio investment transactions, however, also exposed these and other countries to marked financial volatility and recurrent financial panics. The transformation in hemispheric international economic relations—and specifically in U.S. economic relations with the rest of the hemisphere—was already far-reaching as the twenty-first century began.

These structural economic changes had specific and common impacts on the conduct of international economic diplomacy. All governments in the Americas, large and small, had to develop a cadre of experts who could negotiate concrete technical trade, investment, and other economic issues with the United States and with other countries in the region. All had to create teams of international trade lawyers and experts capable of defending national interests and the interests of particular business firms in international, inter-American, or subregional dispute-resolution panels or "courtlike" proceedings. The discourse and practice of inter-American relations, broadly understood, became much more professional—less the province of eloquent poets, more the domain of number-crunching litigators and mediators.

The changes in Latin America's domestic political regimes began in the late 1970s. These, too, would contribute to change the texture of inter-American relations. By the end of 1990, democratization based on fair elections, competitive parties, constitutionalism, and respect for the rule of law and the liberties of citizens had advanced and was still advancing throughout the region, albeit unevenly and with persisting serious problems, Cuba being the principal exception.

Democratization also affected the international relations of Latin American and Caribbean countries, albeit in more subtle ways. The Anglophone Caribbean is a largely archipelagic region long marked by the widespread practice of constitutional government. Since the 1970s, Anglophone Caribbean democratic governments rallied repeatedly to defend constitutional government on any of the islands where it came under threat and, in the specific cases of Grenada and Guyana, to assist the process of democratization in the 1980s and 1990s respectively. In the 1990s, Latin American governments began to act collectively as well to defend and promote democratic rule; with varying degrees of success they did so—with U.S. support—in Guatemala, Haiti, Paraguay, and Peru. Democratization had a more complex relationship to the content of specific foreign policies. In the 1990s, democratization in Argentina, Brazil, Uruguay, and Chile, on balance, contributed to improved international political, security, and economic relations among these southern cone countries. Yet democratic politics at times made it more difficult to manage international relations over boundary or territorial issues between given pairs of countries, including Chile and Peru, Colombia and Venezuela, and Costa Rica and Nicaragua. In general, democratization facilitated better relations between Latin American and Caribbean countries, on the one hand, and the United States, on the other. Across the Americas, democratic governments, including the United States and Canada, acted to defend and promote constitutional government. Much cooperation over security, including the attempt to foster cooperative security and civilian supremacy over the military, would have been unthinkable except in the new, deeper, democratic context in the hemisphere.

At its best, in the 1990s democratic politics made it possible to transform the foreign policies of particular presidential administrations into the foreign policies of states. For example, Argentina's principal political parties endorsed the broad outlines of their nation's foreign policy, including the framework to govern much friendlier Argentine relations with the United States. All Chilean political parties were strongly committed to their country's transformation into an international trading state. The principal political parties of the Anglophone Caribbean sustained consistent long-lasting foreign policies across different partisan administrations. Mexico's three leading political parties agreed, even if they differed on specifics, that the North American Free Trade Agreement should be implemented, binding Mexico to the United States and Canada. And the Bush and Clinton administrations in the United States followed remarkably compatible policies toward Latin America and the Caribbean with regard to the promotion of free trade, pacification in Central America, support for international financial institutions, and the defense of constitutional government in Latin America and the Caribbean. Both administrations acted in concert with other states in the region and often through the Organization of American States. Democratic procedures, in these and other cases, served to establish the credibility of a state's foreign policy because all actors would have reason to expect that the framework of today's foreign policy would endure tomorrow.

The end of the Cold War in Europe began following the accession of Mikhail Gorbachev to the post of General-Secretary of the Communist Party of the Soviet Union in 1985. It accelerated during the second half of the 1980s, culminating with the collapse of communist regimes in Europe between 1989 and 1991 and the breakup of the Soviet Union itself in late 1991. The impact of the end of the U.S.-Soviet conflict on the hemisphere was subtle but important: the United States was no longer obsessed with the threat of communism. Freed to focus on other international interests, the United States discovered that it shared many practical interests with Latin American and Caribbean countries; the latter, in turn, found it easier to cooperate with the United States. There was one exception to this "benign" international process. The United States was also freed to forget its long-lasting fear of communist guerrillas in Colombia (who remained powerful and continued to operate nonetheless) in order to concentrate on a "war" against drug trafficking, even if it undermined Colombia's constitutional regime.

This process of the end of the Cold War had also a specific component in the Western Hemisphere, namely, the termination of the civil and international wars that had swirled in Central America since the late 1970s. The causes of those wars had been internal and international. In the early 1990s, the collapse of the Soviet Union and the marked weakening of Cuban influence enabled the U.S. government to support negotiations with governments or insurgent movements it had long opposed. All of these international changes made it easier to arrange for domestic political, military, and social settlements of the wars in and around Nicaragua, El Salvador, and Guatemala. The end of the Cold War in Europe had an extraordinary impact on Cuba as well. The Cold War did not end the sharp conflict between the U.S. and Cuban governments, but the latter was deprived of Soviet support, forcing it thereby to recall its troops overseas, open its economy to the world, and lower its foreign policy profile. The United States felt freer to conduct a "Colder War" against Cuba, seeking to overthrow its government.

Two other large-scale processes, connected to the previous three, had a significant impact in the international relations of the Western Hemisphere. They were the booms in international migration and in cocaine-related international organized crime. To be sure, emigration and organized crime on an international scale in the Americas are as old as the European settlement begun in the late fifteenth century and the growth of state-sponsored piracy in the sixteenth century. Yet the volume and acceleration of these two processes in the 1980s and 1990s were truly extraordinary.

One effect of widespread violence in Central America and in Colombia, and of the economic depression everywhere, was to accelerate the rate of emigration to the United States. Once begun, the process of migration to the United States was sustained through networks of relatives and friends, the family-unification provisions of U.S. legislation, and the lower relative costs of more frequent international transportation and communication. By the mid-1990s, over twelve million people born in Latin America resided in the United States; two thirds of them had arrived since 1980. The number of Latin American–ancestry people in the United States was much larger, of course. In the 1980s, migrants came to the United States not just from countries of traditional emigration, such as Mexico, but also from countries that in the past had generated few emigrants, such as Brazil. As the twentieth century ended, more persons born in Latin America lived in the United States than lived in the majority of the Latin American states. The United States had also come to play a major role in the production and consumption of the culture of the Spanish-speaking peoples, including music, book publishing, and television programming. These trends are likely to intensify in the twenty-first century.

Had this series of books been published in the mid-1970s, coca and cocaine would have merited brief mention in one or two books, and no mention in most. The boom in U.S. cocaine consumption in the late 1970s and 1980s changed this. The regionwide economic collapse of the 1980s made it easier to bribe public officials, judges, police, and military officers. U.S. cocaine supply interdiction policies in the 1980s raised the price of cocaine, making the coca and cocaine businesses the most lucrative in depression-ravaged economies. The generally unregulated sale of weapons in the United States equipped gangsters throughout the Americas. Bolivia and Peru produced the coca. Colombians grew it, refined it, and financed it. Criminal gangs in the Caribbean, Central America, and Mexico transported and distributed it. Everywhere, drug traffic–related violence and corruption escalated.

The impact of economic policy change, democratization, and the end of the Cold War in Europe on U.S.–Latin American relations, therefore, provides important explanations common to the countries of the Americas in their relations with the United States. The acceleration of emigration and the construction and development of international organized crime around the cocaine business are also key common themes in the continent's international relations during the closing two decades of the twentieth century. To the extent pertinent, these topics appear in each of the books in this series. Nonetheless, each country's own history, geographic location, set of neighbors, resource endowment, institutional features, and leadership characteristics bear as well on the construction, design, and implementation of its foreign policy. These more particular factors enrich and guide the books in this series in their interplay with the more general arguments.

As the 1990s ended, dark clouds reappeared on the firmament of inter-American relations, raising doubts about the "optimistic" trajectory that seemed set at the beginning of that decade. The role of the military in the running of state agencies and activities that normally belong to civilians rose significantly in Colombia,

Venezuela, and Peru, and in January 2000 a military coup overthrew the constitutionally elected president of Ecuador; serious concerns resurfaced concerning the depth and durability of democratic institutions and practices in these countries. Venezuela seemed ready once again to try much heavier government involvement in economic affairs. And the United States had held back from implementing the commitment to hemispheric free trade that both Presidents Bush and Clinton had pledged. Only the last of these trends had instant international repercussions, but all of them could adversely affect the future of a Western Hemisphere based on free politics, free markets, and peace.

This Project

Each of the books in the series has two authors, typically one from a Latin American or Caribbean country and another from the United States (and, in one case, the United Kingdom). We chose this approach to facilitate the writing of the books and also to ensure that the books would represent the international perspectives from both sides of the U.S.–Latin American relationship. In addition, we sought to embed each book within international networks of scholarly work in more than one country.

We have attempted to write short books that ask common questions to enable various readers—scholars, students, public officials, international entrepreneurs, and the educated public—to make their own comparisons and judgments as they read two or more volumes in the series. The project sought to foster comparability across the books through two conferences held at the Instituto Tecnológico Autónomo de México (ITAM) in Mexico City. The first, held in June 1998, compared ideas and questions; the second, held in August 1999, discussed preliminary drafts of the books. Both of us read and commented on all the manuscripts; the manuscripts also received commentary from other authors in the project. We also hope that the network of scholars created for this project will continue to function, even if informally, and that the Web page created for this project will provide for a wider audience access to the ideas, research, and writing associated with it.

We are grateful to the Ford Foundation for its principal support of this project, and to Cristina Eguizábal for her advice and assistance throughout this endeavor. We are also grateful to the MacArthur Foundation for the support that made it possible to hold a second successful project conference in Mexico City. The Rockefeller Foundation provided the two of us with an opportunity to spend four splendid weeks in Bellagio, Italy, working on our various general responsibilities in this project. The Academic Department of International Studies at ITAM hosted the project throughout its duration and the two international conferences. We appreciate the support of the Asociación Mexicana de Cultura, ITAM's principal supporter in this work. Harvard University's Weatherhead Center for International Affairs also supported aspects of this project, as did Harvard University's David Rockefeller Center for Latin American Studies. We are particularly grateful to Hazel Blackmore and Juana Gómez at ITAM, and Amanda Pearson and Kathleen Hoover at the Weatherhead Center, for their work on many aspects of the project. At Routledge, Melissa Rosati encouraged us from the start; Eric Nelson supported the project through its conclusion.

Jorge I. Domínguez
HARVARD UNIVERSITY

Rafael Fernández de Castro
ITAM

PREFACE

THE RELATIONSHIP BETWEEN CHILE AND THE UNITED States has many unique characteristics in the U.S.–Latin American context. In the nineteenth century, Chile had been an important rival to U.S. pretensions on the Pacific coast of South America. Even as a status quo power in the twentieth century, Chile found itself in important disagreement with the United States whenever the latter attempted to mold the hemisphere to its liking. In short, Chilean foreign policy choices, by governments from both the left and the right of the political spectrum, contributed to a bilateral political and military relationship characterized by a high degree of conflict. After Cuba, Chile experienced the longest period of extreme stress with the regional superpower in this century, from 1969 to 1989.

Since the end of the Cold War, although not directly linked to the ending of the superpower confrontation, the Chilean-U.S. relationship has improved dramatically. Chile came reasonably close to becoming the Latin American nation, after Mexico, with the most formalized economic integration with the United States. Although the U.S. Congress blocked Chilean accession to the North American Free Trade Agreement, no other Latin American nation has made it that far in the process. Chile is seen by the United States as a model for Latin America, both in its economic reforms as well as in some aspects of its military policies (e.g., production of the first Defense White Paper in Latin America), though not in others (e.g., the extent of military prerogatives).

This book examines the Chilean-U.S. relationship since the end of the Cold War both to document the dramatic improvement in bilateral relations and to explain this evolution. We argue that this relationship is unique largely because Chilean political, economic, and ideological dependence upon the United States is low. Because Chile wants or needs little from the United States, it has a greater degree of maneuverability in its relationship with the United States than is the norm in Latin America. Chilean society as a whole, and consequently the governments that have represented the different sectors of that society, has been unafraid of the consequences of disagreeing with the United States on some very important issues. These include human rights, civil-military relations, and arms procurement policies.

This relative independence means that when Chile chooses to cooperate with the United States on a bilateral or regional basis, it is doing so because such cooperation plays a role in Chile's national development strategy, not because it reluctantly bows to superior U.S. pressure. As a result, Chile will also be a more willing advocate of some modifications in U.S. policy preferences for the hemisphere. This current coincidence of Chilean and U.S. interests on many hemispheric policies bodes well for cooperation. It also cautions us to expect disagreements between the two that will call for U.S. accommodation if the bilateral relationship is to continue being friendly and fruitful as the hemisphere confronts future challenges to its peace and well-being.

Organization of the Book

The integration of international, domestic, and transnational variables opens up some policy options while closing others. Hence we have organized this book by analyzing first how each variable has affected each country individually. The impact on each country then helps us understand the evolution of the bilateral relationship. It will be important, however, to recognize that in the bilateral relationship the variables may be directly causal, may serve as catalysts, or may be merely coincident, depending upon the issue at hand.

This book is organized into an Introduction with one chapter, two analytical sections with five chapters, and a Postscript. The historical and contemporary material in Chapter One provides a lead-in to the subsequent chapters of the first section. An intense rivalry in the nineteenth century and a less-strained competition in the first half of the twentieth century characterized the historical relationship. There was a short period of increasing cooperation during the 1960s, which was then abruptly derailed with the ascension of the Allende and Pinochet governments.

The first section, "Foreign Policy Decision-Making in the Relationship," examines the international, domestic, and transnational factors at work in the bilateral relationship. Chapter Two focuses on the international factors that influence the relationship between Chile and the United States. These factors are divided into three types. First are those occurring at the deep structural level of the international system: both politicomilitary events such as the end of bipolarity (the Cold War) as well as the accelerated process of economic globalization. We also examine the growing importance of international institutions in the 1990s on the political, economic, and social relationships between these two countries.

Chapter Three investigates the domestic factors that influence decision-making in the two countries. These domestic factors will keep some things off the bilateral agenda, make others easier to solve, and make still other items difficult to address. Intergovernmental factors and the general political debates within each country can affect the bilateral relationship. For example, a policy option that might strengthen the relationship might not be chosen because one of the branches of government is feuding with another, rather than because of a disagreement on the merits of the policy itself.

Chapter Four complements the analysis of the previous two chapters with an examination of transnational relations between the two societies. The transnational corporations that invested in Chile had always affected U.S.-Chilean relations. But the politicization of the Allende and Pinochet years stimulated numerous new points of contact between the two societies. Structural economic reforms in Chile also produced new links among businessmen in the two societies and gave nongovernmental organizations (NGOs) a new issue (inequality and poverty) upon which to focus once democracy had returned to Chile. These interactions among nongovernmental actors can facilitate or impede government action. One of the interesting aspects of the Chilean-U.S. relationship is that this transnationalization of societies may be pulling the two societies farther apart rather than closer together.

The second section of the book we have titled "The Maturing (?) of the Chilean–United States Relationship" in recognition of the continuing potential for disagreement on major national goals. It is divided into two chapters, one for each Chilean administration since redemocratization, because the task for each was somewhat different. In each period we analyze the effects of the interaction of international, domestic, and transnational variables on the evolution of the bilateral relationship.

Chapter Five, "Reestablishing Cooperative Relations: The Aylwin Administration," examines the efforts by the new democratic government to build a cooperative relationship with the United States. The transition to democracy did not automatically resolve some of the disputes peculiar to the military regime, such as the Letelier case. Goodwill alone did not guarantee that a satisfactory solution for both sides would be reached in outstanding disputes like that in the poisoned grapes case. The Chile-U.S. relationship in the economic sphere would have to find its place on the U.S. agenda for the hemisphere. Unfortunately, U.S. consideration of a free trade agreement with Chile was postponed while the U.S. Congress dealt with Mexico's accession to the North American Free Trade Agreement.

Eduardo Frei Ruiz-Tagle's administration represented a major step forward for Chile's democracy. Chapter Six examines bilateral relations in the military and economic realms. There were clearly issues of important disagreement that in the past might have truncated the move toward cooperation. The United States was insensitive to Chile's defense paradigm and continued to keep a free trade treaty just out of reach. But the Frei administration responded in a manner that continued to decrease Chile's vulnerability to the United States without provoking it.

In the Postscript we step beyond the specifics of the Chile-U.S. relationship to discern the lessons of this relationship for our understanding of U.S.–Latin American relations in general. We argue that foreign policy analysis in all countries of the hemisphere should seek to understand how international, national, and transnational factors produce policy goals for each country, the policies adopted by each to reach those goals (individually or cooperatively), and the results of the implementation of those policies. The Postscript chapter examines the first half-year of the administration of Ricardo Lagos in 2000.

Acknowledgments

We have benefited greatly from comments by series editors Rafael Fernández de Castro and Jorge I. Domínguez, as well as those from participants at two workshops held at the Instituto Tecnológico Autónomo de México. David Mares thanks the University of California Pacific Rim Research Program for providing partial funding to investigate Chile's economic relations with the United States. We thank an anonymous reviewer and Eric Nelson of Routledge for their comments and encouragement. We are especially grateful to FLACSO-Chile's bibliographic team for providing us with a wealth of information and tolerating our constant demand for more.

INTRODUCTION

ONE

HISTORICAL CHARACTERISTICS OF THE BILATERAL RELATIONSHIP: CONTINUITIES AND CHANGES

CHILE AND THE UNITED STATES HAVE A LONG HISTORY of engagement, starting in the nineteenth century when two ambitious nascent powers competed in power projection and development of rival naval capabilities. These interstate issues were well understood by policy-makers on both sides, and they avoided outright confrontation. Even as Chile lost the ability to compete with the United States, Chilean policy-makers found ways to advance Chilean national interests without creating a crisis in the relationship. Until the 1960s, therefore, the bilateral relationship was characterized by tense competition and limited but growing cooperation.

The 1960s represented a watershed in the binational relationship. In the early 1960s, the two countries responded very differently to the Cuban Revolution. The U.S. response is well known: to draw a line in the sand that other countries would cross at their peril. Internationally, Chile urged nonintervention. Domestically, recognizing her own vulnerability to the social and economic issues that encouraged Castro, Chile focused on reform. By the late 1960s the shape that reform took in Chile threatened to violate the ideological rules that the United States aggressively policed in the wake of the Cuban Revolution. The separation between international and domestic politics that had formed the basis upon which the relationship had been successfully managed broke down. Identifying each other as threats, the administrations of Richard Nixon and Salvador Allende polarized the relationship, with the former using covert aid to subvert the latter. The administrations of Gerald Ford (1973–1976) and Ronald Reagan (1980–1988) initially attempted to accommodate the military government that overthrew Allende. But the U.S. Congress and later Jimmy Carter's administration (1976–1980) continually clashed with General Augusto Pinochet over human rights and redemocratization, precluding any normalization of relations until the return of democracy in 1990.

After 1990 a new basis for managing cooperative relations emerged. International and domestic politics were still linked, but on terms that differed from the earlier period. Both Chile and the United States agreed that international politics now focused on economic rather than security matters, and domestic politics had to be democratic and respectful of human rights. Under these new terms both parties have been able to keep conflict over specific issues from threatening the generally cooperative character of their relationship.

This chapter has four parts and a conclusion. We begin with a summary of the historical relationship from Chile's independence to the early response of the United States to the Cuban Revolution. The subsequent section begins with high hopes of cooperation under the banner of socioeconomic reform, which are quickly dashed in the open confrontations between the United States and first the Popular Unity government (1970–1973) and then the military dictatorship (1973–1990). Our third section provides an overview of the changes and continuities in the Chile-U.S. relationship since the return of democracy in 1990. The final section utilizes a brief discussion concerning the impact of the end of the Cold War upon the bilateral relationship to set the stage for analyzing contemporary Chilean-U.S. relations. In the conclusion we underscore the challenges and opportunities that the bilateral relationship would have to face in the 1990s and beyond.

A History of Managed Competition and Tensions, 1812–1962

After the wars of independence, Chile and Paraguay were the first Spanish-American colonies to establish stable central governments that could organize politics and create a context for productive investment. At the same time, the governments could extract resources from society to support domestic and foreign policy. This capability gave them an advantage in dealing with their South American neighbors.

Paraguay, however, lost its bid for dominance in the Paraguay/Rio de la Plata basin as the result of a long and bloody war against Argentina, Brazil, and Uruguay in the War of the Triple Alliance. Chile, on the other hand, defeated the alliance that challenged its supremacy on the Pacific Coast in the War of the Peruvian-Bolivian Confederation (1836–1839) and the War of the Pacific (1879–1884, again against Peru and Bolivia) and cultivated relations with Ecuador, which had its own territorial dispute with Peru.

While Chile was harnessing its political power and economic wealth in a bid for subregional dominance, the United States was engaged in very similar efforts in North America and the Caribbean. Its westward movement and despoliation of Mexico in the 1830s and 1840s caused the Chilean minister to the United States to remark: "What today they are doing to Mexico by taking over California, they will do to us tomorrow for frivolous reasons if it occurs to them." After Mexico, the United States turned to Central America and the Caribbean. The U.S. call for a hemispheric conference in 1889 and Secretary of State Richard Olney's declaration in 1895 to the British that the U.S. word was "practically fiat" in the hemisphere demonstrated that South America fell within the self-defined scope of U.S. interests.

These two trajectories toward major power status on the west coast of South America put Chile and the United States on a course of competing interests. When the United States attempted to buy all the rights to guano in Ecuador's Galapagos Islands in 1854, Chile tried to rally Latin American and European cooperation to stop U.S. expansion. The U.S. minister in Santiago noted in 1859 that Chileans feared that the United States was planning forcibly to annex Mexico and the other Latin American states. One of the major newspapers, *El Mercurio*, saw the United States as a "threat to everything that you touch and surrounds you because you cannot live for much time in peace. This is the danger for Chile and all of the Spanish American republics." The paper warned that Chile must become a developed state like the United States or face the same fate as Mexico.[1]

The War of the Pacific (1879–1884), in which Chile gained important territory and resources in the north, brought the two countries directly into opposition. The United States attempted to mediate the conflict and prevent Chile from enjoying the fruits of victory. However, Chile's fleet intimidated the United States. As negotiations broke down, and with the U.S. naval presence in the Peruvian port of Callao, Admiral Patricio Lynch seized the Peruvian president and shipped him off to Chile on the battleship *Cochrane*. One of the U.S. officers, Alfred T. Mahan, sorely lamented having been sent on a mission with ships that were a "laughing stock" and that damaged U.S. pride and self-esteem. (Mahan shortly thereafter became the chief architect of the U.S. naval program that turned the United States into a world power.)[2]

Chile's regional influence continued to increase after its victory in the War of the Pacific. More ironclads were added to modernize the fleet, augmenting the power of the Chilean Navy. The U.S. *Army and Navy Journal*, for example, noted that the battleship *Esmeralda* "could destroy our entire Navy, ship by ship, and never be touched." U.S. congressmen worried that Chile's reach could extend to California and Oregon.[3]

In 1885, when the U.S. Navy responded to unrest by temporarily occupying the city of Colón in Panama, Colombia requested aid in putting down the rebellion before the United States could support it. Chile sent the *Esmeralda* to Panama with orders to prevent U.S. annexation of Panama. Chilean forces disembarked on the isthmus and did not leave until the United States evacuated Colón. Chile also competed with the United States for influence in Ecuador, sending the *Esmeralda* to Guayaquil as a demonstration of its interests. Arguably, the crowning glory of this postwar period of expanding Chilean influence was the annexation of Easter Island, 2,700 miles to the west, in 1888.[4]

The 1890s were a decade in which Chile discovered that it was reaching the limits of its power potential while its competitors, Argentina and the United States, were accelerating their upward trajectories. In 1891 the political stability that had helped Chile become powerful collapsed in civil war. Argentina grew demographically and economically while developing a more stable polity. By 1890 the United States, with five battleships larger than the *Esmeralda*, became a major naval power.

Proof of the important changes in the bilateral relationship surfaced when the United States and Chile became embroiled in a serious dispute. On the night of October 16, 1891, a barroom fight escalated into a near-riot and the death of two sailors from the USS *Baltimore*. Disagreements left over from the War of the Pacific and the Chilean civil war of 1891 fueled tensions to the point that the United States sent two cruisers to Chile and Congress authorized war "if necessary" to defend U.S. honor and prestige. Argentina provided the United States with information on Chile's military capabilities and offered the use of its own territory to aid U.S. soldiers in an attack on Chile. Chile ultimately worked out a face-saving diplomatic solution in the *Baltimore* affair, but it was clear that power had shifted away from Chile.[5]

Chile responded quickly to the new geopolitical situation, revising its foreign policy to become a status quo power forced to rely on strategic cooperation with other countries to counter U.S. influence and further its own interests. The lingering issues from the War of the Pacific were Bolivia's insistence on restoration of an outlet to the sea, and the future of the cities of Tacna and Arica, previously part of Peru. Bolivia and Peru sought the intervention of the League of Nations and the United States to settle the disputes. When Peru subsequently withdrew the request to the League because the United States opposed League involvement, Chile tried to head off U.S. involvement by reopening bilateral negotiations. Chile also tried enticing Japan and Britain in a trade of Easter Island for armaments and diplomatic support for Chile's position on Tacna-Arica; but neither extrahemispheric great power was interested. In 1929 Peru and Chile agreed in bilateral negotiations to split the difference (Peru got Tacna, Chile kept Arica).[6]

Within a decade the United States and Chile clashed over another foreign policy issue. As the winds of war began to engulf Europe and Asia, the United States sought to develop hemispheric unity behind U.S. policy. The first step was to gain agreement to consult before any state adopted a policy in the event of war. The 1936 Pan-American conference at Buenos Aires provided this agreement. Within two years the United States sought a mutual defense pact within the hemisphere, but Chile and others worried about the implications of agreeing to adopt automatically a particular foreign policy. The 1938 Lima conference of American states limited itself to reaffirming continental solidarity and the agreement to consult. At the beginning of the European war, American foreign ministers met at Panama to discuss continental policy. Because the United States wanted to keep the hemisphere out of the war, the meeting adopted a General Declaration of Neutrality.[7]

Chile supported neutrality for domestic and international reasons. Many Chileans were of German or Italian ancestry and maintained sympathies for their former countrymen. As a democracy, Chilean politicians also worried about potential electoral costs of taking sides in a distant war. An additional important factor was Germany's status as Chile's major trading partner because of special trading agreements spurred by the collapse of the global trading system during the Depression.[8] Consequently, from 1936 to 1939, U.S. and Chilean policy coincided because their interests coincided.

Once the Low Countries and France fell to the Germans, and England became a potential victim, U.S. policy shifted. Despite its official neutrality, the United States began to provide the British with aid. U.S. interests completed their 180 degree turnabout after the Japanese attack on Pearl Harbor. A month after entering the war in both Asia and Europe (and without consulting Latin American governments, despite the previous inter-American agreements), the United States tried to get Latin America to sever relations with the Axis powers. The symbolic value of a hemisphere unified against the Axis was enormous to the United States.

Japan's attack on the United States and the developing war in Europe did not change Chile's foreign policy. To the prior domestic reasons for neutrality was added a well-founded concern, shared by the U.S. War Department, that the United States could not convincingly defend Chile should Japan attack.[9]

Chile initially resisted breaking relations with the Axis, though it did sell copper to the United States at below open market prices and purchased gasoline and obsolete military equipment under the U.S. Lend-Lease program. After a year of strained relations with the United States, Chile severed relations with the Axis. Though the United States was still not content with Chilean efforts to counter Axis espionage and propaganda, Chile took no definitive action until the Soviet Union demanded participation in the war as a precondition for joining the United Nations. Only then, in February 1945, did Chile symbolically declare war against Germany.[10]

From the end of World War II until the early 1960s, Chilean and U.S. security interests began converging as both countries made the fight against communism a priority. Chile signed the Inter-American Treaty of Reciprocal Assistance in 1947 and later a bilateral military assistance agreement with the United States. Chile supported U.S. actions in overthrowing the government in Guatemala in 1954 and voted consistently with the United States in the United Nations.

Disagreements persisted in the economic arena. Although the United States provided some economic aid, it refused to accept the concept of a Marshall Plan for Latin America, as advocated by Chile and other Latin American countries. Chile's continued pressure on the U.S. copper companies to pay higher prices and taxes also produced points of friction with the U.S. government.[11] Neither country, however, was interested in allowing these irritations to escalate to a point that would harm the relationship.

The Relationship under Stress, 1962–1990

Bilateral relations began to deteriorate as Chilean domestic politics polarized and U.S. anticommunist efforts moved in new directions after the Cuban Revolution. Fidel Castro's victory provided a new stimulus for further legal and illegal efforts by the left to promote change throughout the hemisphere. The United States responded by attempting to overthrow the Cuban government and, failing that, to isolate it. By supporting new regional policies, including the Alliance for Progress, the United States helped to promote socioeconomic change and shore up Latin American governments. After a successful but embarrassing U.S. military intervention in the Dominican Republic, the United States advocated new mechanisms by which the Organization of American States (OAS) could intervene in a country facing communist revolution.

Chile's political elites were unhappy with these new U.S. policies for the hemisphere. The conservative government of Jorge Alessandri (1958–1964) opposed the violation of sovereignty inherent in U.S. proposals for the OAS. It abstained from the 1962 votes to suspend Cuba from the OAS, to end weapons sales to Cuba, and to consider imposing sanctions. Although later in the year it agreed with the U.S. condemnation of nuclear missiles in Cuba, Chile joined Mexico in demanding that any intervention to remove the missiles not be used to depose the Cuban government. In 1964 the Alessandri government also abstained on the vote to sanction Cuba, although as a member of the OAS it agreed to abide by the organization's decisions. And at home, the conservative elites opposed many of the reforms, especially land reform, promoted by the new U.S. anticommunist policies.[12]

Allende's near-victory in the 1958 presidential elections frightened the U.S. government as well as Chile's center and right. The U.S. strategy of social and economic reform to combat communism made it a natural ally of the center party in Chile, the Christian Democrats (Partido Demócrata Cristiano, PDC). Under President Lyndon B. Johnson the CIA covertly channeled three million dollars to the campaign of PDC candidate Eduardo Frei in order to avoid a victory by Allende in the 1964 election.[13]

The Frei administration sought to establish a "revolution of liberty" based on the idea of "integrated democracy." This concept of democracy was based upon three basic principles: a focus on people as the subject of government policy (Christian humanism); an elite perspective aimed at improving the situation of people living on the social and economic margins of society; and support of democratic institutions.[14]

Accomplishing this dramatic change seemed to require making the economy develop according to national, rather than international, priorities. The Frei administration pushed agrarian reform and the Chileanization of copper, a process through which the Chilean state would purchase 51 percent of the shares of foreign-owned mines. Latin American integration was another issue of great importance to Frei, just as it was to become for Salvador Allende.

The Frei administration proved unwilling in some cases and unable in others to safeguard U.S. interests. In the wake of the Dominican invasion, Frei refused to support U.S. efforts to provide the OAS with the ability to intervene in the internal affairs of its member countries. Frei universalized diplomatic relations, establishing links with the Soviet Union and other central and eastern European countries, although relations with Cuba were not reestablished.[15] The U.S. firm Anaconda refused to accept "Chileanization" and appealed to the U.S. government for support. The United States, however, continued to support Frei through the Alliance for Progress and pressured Anaconda to sell.

Between 1964 and 1970 Chile experienced important progress in the social, cultural, economic, and political spheres. The initial successes of the Christian Democrats in generating a humane national capitalist system made Frei's agenda appear to offer an alternative to the Cuban revolution. The tensions unleashed by these important changes, however, began to fray the commitments of some social forces to Chile's democratic institutions. Even civil-military relations started becoming tense. In 1969, for example, the "Tacna" military regiment expressed its concern by refusing to leave its barracks.[16]

Ultimately, Frei was unable to get far-reaching reforms through Congress or, for those that did pass the legislature, implement them on a major scale. Frei's inability to make progress toward a broad-based national development sapped the political strength of the center. The PDC suffered defections from its progressive wing toward the left after 1967, and a portion of its constituency even moved to the right. For the 1970 elections, Jorge Alessandri was supported by the National Party and other forces on the right. The PDC nominated Radomiro Tomic, who represented the party's left wing. With his opposition divided, Allende won a narrow plurality in the election.[17]

Chilean-U.S. relations were dramatically restructured when Allende was elected president. Although Allende was a member of the Socialist Party, the Nixon administration considered his government to be "communist." Unlike the People's Republic of China or Yugoslavia, two communist countries with which the United States had good relations in the 1970s, Chile could offer no strategic advantages to the United States that could offset their ideological differences. The Nixon administration, consequently, could see few nuances in the makeup of the Allende administration that might make accommodation possible. Conflict was the result.

U.S. covert action continued after the election. Since the Chilean Congress had to ratify the winner if no candidate received a majority of the vote, the United States tried to influence legislators to vote for one of the other two candidates. The CIA also explored the possibility of a military coup to prevent Allende from taking office, followed by new elections, presumably to preserve "democracy." U.S. Ambassador Edward M. Korry opposed a military coup because he thought it could not succeed, partly because the military high command had no desire to become involved in politics. His favored approach was economic sanctions; he told Frei that should Allende assume the presidency ". . . not a nut or bolt will be allowed to reach Chile under Allende . . . we shall do all in our power to condemn Chile and Chileans to utmost deprivation and poverty."[18]

Alessandri provided the PDC senators with an enticing offer as well: he promised to resign immediately and call new elections if the Congress confirmed him as victor. This procedure would allow Frei, constitutionally forbidden from running for consecutive terms, to run for president. Given the recent electoral results, it was clear that the center-right would throw its support behind Frei, guaranteeing his election.

Allende and the left threatened to immobilize the country if the plurality winner was not confirmed, as was the tradition. The PDC settled for demanding that Allende and his Popular Unity Coalition accept constitutional reforms guaranteeing the professionalization of the military and freedom of the press. After the Congress approved these amendments, it proceeded to ratify Allende's victory.[19]

The election of Allende meant many different things to different sectors of society and the state. Many people on the left wanted what they considered a "real democracy" rather than the "formal democracy" that existed. This meant that democracy should empower all people and address their demands, especially in the economic arena. Changing the character of the state became a primary objective for grassroots organizations and movements on the left, provoking a reaction by social forces on the center and right. Issues of governability and the legitimacy of institutions began to dog the political system. The political class was polarized and unable to establish even the most minor accords needed for reaching democratic solutions.[20] This process would culminate in the rupturing of constitutional order.

The basic tenets of Chilean foreign policy did not change under Allende. Rather, Allende pursued Frei's universalization of diplomatic relations program to its ultimate consequences.[21] This meant consolidating the principle of nonintervention and self-determination, respecting all political systems, and lowering ideological barriers between countries. Allende consequently established relations with Cuba, the People's Republic of China, North Korea, North Vietnam, the Democratic Republic of Germany, and other socialist countries.[22]

Relations between the governments of Chile and the United States deteriorated dramatically between 1970 and 1973. Allende's foreign policy obviously clashed with the Cold War view of "us versus them." Another major point of contention developed after the Chilean Congress unanimously approved legislation nationalizing foreign-owned (mainly U.S.) copper companies. The right supported these nationalizations as repayment for U.S. support of agrarian reform. Allende and his supporters believed that only by freely disposing of its natural resources could Chile advance toward political liberty and win its second independence, that is, economic independence. Allende's administration interpreted the compensation formula in a manner that subtracted excess profits by foreign firms in the past from the amount due them from the nationalization. The result was effectively zero compensation.[23] The U.S. government saw this as merely a scheme to justify an attack on private property and indicative of the "communist" tendencies of Allende's government.

Allende may have sought a nonaligned foreign policy, but the rhetoric of the left-wing members in his congressional coalition was decidedly anti-U.S. In addition, Allende found it difficult to control the behavior of some peasants, workers, and intellectuals who sought to implement far-reaching revolutionary change

TABLE 1.1

Details of U.S. Economic Assistance to Chile and from Multilateral Funds during the Governments of Frei, Allende, and Pinochet (in $U.S. millions)

	Frei (1964–1970)	Allende (1971–1973)	First three years of Pinochet (1974–1976)
US: Direct Economic Aid	397.5	3.3	41.3
US: P.L. 480 (Titles I and II)	108.6	14.7	122.6
US: Military Aid	52.5	33.0	18.5
US: Export-Import Bank	278.0	4.7	141.4
World Bank	131.5	0.0	66.5
Interamerican Development Bank (IDB)	208.7	11.6	237.8
TOTAL	**1,176.8**	**67.3**	**628.1**

Source: Compilation of diverse publications by the State Department, World Bank, and Interamerican Development Bank.

quickly and before their electoral moment had passed. The U.S. covert operation against Allende's government found ready allies within Chile among those frightened at the prospect of socialist revolution.[24]

Political polarization, economic chaos, and the U.S. embargo (also known as the "Invisible Blockade") finally stimulated the Chilean military to overthrow Allende's government. In retrospect, the political and economic program of the Allende government did not adequately appreciate the extreme reaction of the United States nor its own vulnerabilities. Furthermore, the doctrine of nonalignment, though it helped Chile in the Third World arena, did not contribute to deepening its ties to Europe and this could not counterbalance the U.S. reaction.

Relations between Chile and the executive branch of the U. S. government initially improved after the overthrow of Allende in 1973. The military junta was clearly anticommunist and soon became promarket as well. Although it did not reverse the copper nationalizations, the junta did pay compensation. The Nixon administration responded by opening up the channels for economic assistance. During the three years of the Allende government, official U.S. and multilateral financial assistance totaled 67.3 million dollars; it reached 628.1 million dollars for the first three years of the Pinochet regime, which represented a level slightly ahead of that granted the Frei government (see Table 1.1).[25]

The Chilean military fared less well with Congress and the U.S. public. The military government's early and stark abuses of human rights mobilized activists in the United States and alienated important voices in Congress. Public opinion polls revealed that in 1975 approximately 60 percent of the U.S. public believed that Chileans had lived better under Allende's government.[26] In early 1976 the

U.S. Congress adopted the Kennedy-Humphrey Amendment, suspending sales of arms to Chile and limiting economic aid to the Chilean military regime because of the human rights abuses in Chile.[27] The amendment permitted arms sales and more economic aid only when the president certified that "substantial" progress had been made on human rights. Secretary of State Henry Kissinger, an early supporter of the coup and a well-known advocate of the supremacy of national security considerations above all else, ultimately had to warn Pinochet's regime in 1976 about its human rights behavior.[28]

With the election of Jimmy Carter to the U.S. presidency in late 1976, official relations with Chile deteriorated once again because the Carter administration opposed the military government on principle. But the military government's refusal to cooperate fully in the investigation into the assassination by the military government's secret police of Allende's former ambassador to the United States, Orlando Letelier, and a companion in Washington, D.C., brought official relations to their lowest point. Carter canceled Chile's Export-Import Bank loans and insurance by the Overseas Private Investment Corporation, reduced the size of the military mission, and suspended Chilean participation in the annual U.S. naval exercises carried out with South American navies (UNITAS).[29]

Chile became identified as a "pariah state" in the international system as a result of its abuse of human rights and staunch anticommunist foreign relations stance. Chilean diplomacy also took on authoritarian trappings that contrasted with the civilian governments' pragmatic diplomacy that had previously characterized the professionalism of Chilean diplomacy. Many European ambassadors left Chile, and the rupture of diplomatic relations with Mexico was especially important. Isolation increased the country's international vulnerability, especially in border disputes with Peru (1974–1976) and Argentina (1978–1984), and vis-à-vis the United States starting from 1976.[30]

The Chilean government lambasted the United States for interference in its internal affairs. The navy in particular condemned its suspension from the UNITAS exercises, charging that the security of the hemisphere was damaged as a result. The government noted publicly that the measures undertaken by Carter "violated the principles of international law and are, simply, a return to the old practices of North American imperialism in Latin America. . . . it is aggressive and arrogant behavior by a government that reacts with violence and complete injustice against a small and materially weak country in its own hemisphere."[31]

Many analysts expected a change in U.S. policy toward Chile with the election of Ronald Reagan as U.S. president. The Reagan administration did improve relations with numerous governments that had abused human rights, including the Argentine military government before the 1982 Malvinas/Falklands War. The common denominator in the Reagan administration's better relations with authoritarian regimes was a willingness of these governments to help U.S. anticommunist efforts, particularly in Central America.

Chile could not benefit from this thawing of U.S. relations with human rights abusers in the 1980s; with the Kennedy legislation, the U.S. Congress had explicitly singled out Chile. The Reagan administration persuaded Congress to modify its sanctions, but under very stringent terms: the president had to certify that the military government was making significant progress on human rights, that military sales were in the U.S. national interest, that Chile was not aiding international terrorism, and that the military government was cooperating on bringing those involved in the Letelier assassination to justice.[32] Another obstacle to improving relations at this time was that Chile's military government criticized the United States' own commitment and actions against communism. Consequently, Chile was less willing to follow the U.S. lead or make policy changes designed to help the United States fight communism.

The Argentine military government's fiasco in the Malvinas War in 1982, in direct contravention of efforts by the Reagan administration to dissuade armed conflict, ended the possibility of improving U.S.-Chilean relations as long as a military government governed the latter. The Reagan administration grew leery of military governments, even of the anticommunist variety. At the same time, the Cold War began to wind down, to the detriment of leftist ideology,[33] and negotiated settlement of the Central American wars became increasingly likely. The U.S. government responded by emphasizing its ideological commitment to democracy as a way of combating leftist guerrillas in the region and the Sandinista government in Nicaragua. Once again, Chile's government found itself at odds with U.S. policy.

The Reagan administration tried to persuade Chile to catch the wave of democracy spreading through the world. Assistant Undersecretary of State for Latin America James Michel told Congress in March 1985: "if democracy is our principal objective, our policy reflects the entire gamut of U.S. interests in Chile, and it is not formed definitively by one overriding factor." Furthermore, he said, "relations with Chile are facilitated through diplomatic means, with due respect to open diplomacy and other means for realizing United States interests." To achieve U.S. goals, active assistance will be given to:

> parties within the government supporting transition, and parties involved in negotiating with the opposition, so that they can reach consensus on a timetable for the democratic transition. We are disposed to support whatever accords are reached by the Government (of Chile) and various democratic parties that are created through direct conversations. . . . Our capacity to support the transition in Chile depends on maintaining open communication channels with the Government of Chile, as well as with the democratic opposition.[34]

The issue of human rights persisted throughout this whole period. Resolutions condemning Chile's human rights violations passed by the United Nations and the Organization of American States continued to garner great support in the international arena. The United States, however, abstained from votes regarding Chile's human rights situation because U. S. priorities lay elsewhere.

Under the guidance of then-ambassador Harry Barnes, the United States developed diverse political initiatives aimed at promoting democratization without undermining the economic reforms implemented by the military government, which the United States strongly supported. The commercial attaché of the U.S. embassy in Santiago maintained that: "we have supported Chile's financial politics through our participation in the World Bank and International Monetary Fund, and through our influence on commercial banks. This support is apparent in the accords that are presently being implemented, and I believe that this will continue in the future as long as Chile maintains its current economic agenda."[35]

As a practical matter, the United States sought an end to the military government through a negotiated settlement largely based upon the Constitution of 1980, written and voted upon under the military government. Under one of the contested terms of the Constitution, Pinochet was to serve two eight-year terms as president, subject to ratification after his first term ended in 1988. (For a discussion, see Chapter Three.) Pinochet successfully resisted domestic and international calls for elections before the scheduled 1988 referendum, even as relations between Pinochet and the U.S. government were so tense that he accused the CIA of having been involved in the assassination attempt on his life in 1986.[36]

The democratic opposition initially rejected the 1980 Constitution as the institutional structure within which any transition to democracy would occur. But after a few years of futile protest, the democrats compromised. As the plebiscite on Pinochet's second eight-year term approached, political parties and the Catholic Church in Chile worked together with European and U.S. political parties and governments to ensure a free and fair election.

The U.S. House of Representatives declared that "the Chilean government is strongly urged to take the measures necessary for assuring that the Chilean people can express themselves freely, openly, and clearly, in the upcoming plebiscite," and called upon the Chilean government to: "end with states of exception, insure equal and open access to means of communication, provide freedom to gather and associate openly so that citizens and political groups may mount pacific campaigns supporting ideas, permit access to international visitors at election sites and vote-tallying centers, and hold a public tabulation of votes with people from both sectors present."[37] The U.S. Congress channeled over a million dollars through the nonpartisan National Endowment for Democracy to register voters and dispatched consultants to work with the united opposition to promote a "free and fair" vote. The Chilean military government responded to this situation by accusing U.S. authorities of receiving Marxists and of being uninformed about Chile's political circumstances.[38]

Unlike the experience of 1964, when the United States covertly channeled millions of dollars to influence the outcome of the elections, efforts by the National Endowment for Democracy were well publicized. When the "No" forces emerged victorious Pinochet considered stealing the election. But the combined pressure from political mobilization within Chile and foreign governments convinced the commanders of the navy and air force to insist upon recognizing the victory of the opposition. The United States applauded the organization and calm of this electoral process in Chile and insisted on a rapid return to democracy.[39]

In the midst of these efforts to promote a democratic transition, relations between the United States and the military government suffered another setback when the U.S. embassy in Santiago received a warning in March 1989 that Chilean grape exports to the United States had been injected with cyanide. The Food and Drug Administration (FDA) examined some grapes in Philadelphia, found two tainted grapes, and embargoed grape imports from Chile. Chilean growers were furious with the loss of over $300 million, and Pinochet's government suspected a U.S. plot. Chile's growers hired their own investigators in the United States, whose findings disagreed with those of the FDA,[40] further clouding the controversy, which would haunt U.S.-Chilean relations for years to come.

The U.S. government observed the subsequent stage of the democratization process very closely. Doubts existed about certain constitutional mechanisms, especially those permitting the continued personal power of General Pinochet as Commander in Chief of the Army and later his establishment as senator for life. Prior to the actual transfer of governance, between 1988 and 1990, the military government generated a series of laws "tying" the future government to certain authoritarian enclaves in the Constitution. However, in 1989, a plebiscite was held that allowed Chileans to make the Constitution substantially more democratic.[41] Patricio Aylwin, leading the center-left Concertación de Partidos por la Democracia, won a definitive 54 percent of the vote later that year and became Chile's first democratically elected president in twenty years.[42]

The Relationship since 1990

All relationships experience continuities and changes. In this section we note the key aspects of the relationship and pay attention to the continuities and changes that define the relationship in the 1990s.

Continuities

The major continuities in the relationship have occurred in the economic realm and reflect the structural characteristics of the Chilean and U.S. economies as well as the dynamics of the international economy.

Share of Trade

The economic relationship between Chile and the United States enables Chilean nationalists on both the right and left to seek a more independent

TABLE 1.2

Chile's Foreign Trade by Region, 1992 and 1995
(Percent of total imports and exports)

Region	Exports		Imports	
	1992	1995	1992	1995
North America*	16.9	15.0	22.0	26.8
Latin America	16.8	18.8	24.8	26.8
Europe	31.7	29.4	23.5	22.3
Asia	31.1	34.0	18.4	16.9
Rest of the World	3.5	2.8	11.3	7.2

* excluding Mexico

Source: Central Bank of Chile, 1996.

political relationship. From 1981 to 1984 the United States was responsible for 23.3 percent of total Chilean trade. In 1997 the United States and Canada combined represented only 15.7 percent of the value of Chilean exports, a figure roughly similar to that of Japan and below that of the European Union. Chile is slightly more dependent on the import side, with 22 percent of the value of its imports coming from the United States and Canada in 1997.[43] Table 1.2 clearly demonstrates the diversification of Chile's foreign trade.

Share of Direct Foreign Investment

The United States has been the largest foreign investor in Chile, both during the military dictatorship and in the contemporary era. From 1974 to1986 U.S. investors accounted for almost 50 percent of total foreign direct investment, far outdistancing the next major investors at 8 percent (Table 1.3). Yearly figures can fluctuate dramatically, as evidenced by the fact that the U.S. share reached 51 percent in 1995 but had a low of 20.5 percent in 1990. U.S. investors tend to dominate foreign investors in mining, services, and transport and communications, where they account for over 40 percent of total foreign investment, and forestry, with 36.4 percent. These investors are major players in the agricultural, electrical, gas and water, and industrial sectors, with shares ranging from 21 percent to 26 percent. Only in construction (6.1 percent) and fisheries (9.9 percent) are U.S. investors a minor force.[44]

Chileans had not been important foreign investors prior to the structural economic reforms of the military government. These reforms altered the incentives from investing domestically in protected industries to seeking out profitable investments in the foreign sector. The development of regional integration in southern South America at a time when the Chilean stock market was booming produced a flow of Chilean capital that could take advantage of those international opportunities. While U.S. investors dominate capital flows to Chile, Chileans invest their foreign capital elsewhere, as indicated in Table 1.4.

TABLE 1.3

Foreign Investment According to Country of Origin (1974–1986) (millions of $U.S. 1986)

Country	Approved	Percent of Total Approved	Invested	Percent of Total Invested
United States	6,484.83	67.1	1,369.80	49.7
Canada	990.27	10.2	38.60	1.4
Spain	313.50	3.2	234.30	8.5
Great Britain	274.98	2.8	220.50	8.0
Panama	252.02	2.6	162.60	5.9

Source: Secretaría Ejecutiva del Comité de Inversiones Extranjeras.

TABLE 1.4

Chilean Foreign Investments Principal Destinations 1990 to July 1997

Country	Chilean FI	Percent Total Chilean FI
	$U.S. million	
Argentina	5,939.8	43.6
Peru	1,814.8	13.3
Brazil	1,471.0	10.8
Colombia	981.5	7.2
Mexico	499.8	3.7
Panama	387.5	2.8

Source: Comité de Inversiones Extranjeras, *El Mercurio*, February 8, 1998, as cited in Fuentes and Martin, p. 81.

Share of Private Bank Debt

Chile experienced a debt crisis like much of the rest of Latin America in the 1980s. Although Chile's debt was largely in private hands, the military government assumed that debt in order to maintain the country's creditworthiness in international financial markets. Economic reforms implemented after the 1982 collapse provided the basis for a dramatic and sustained period of economic growth, with recession arriving only in 1999. Chile was the most aggressive large debtor country to utilize secondary markets to reduce its debt. By 1993 Chile had lowered its long-term debt by 30 percent through debt conversion and debt-equity swaps. As a result, Chile became attractive once again for voluntary and new private debt.[45]

Changes

The U.S.-Chilean relationship has experienced important changes since 1990. These have been mainly in the political and military arenas, reflecting Chile's return to democracy.

Foreign Policy Process

As a "problem" case, Chile merited special attention from many in U.S. society and government. When U.S. conservatives attacked the Chilean government, U.S. progressives rushed to defend it, and vice versa. At any given time, these political dynamics tended to make Chile a priority for someone in the U.S. Congress or executive. With active partisans in the legislative and executive branches, the foreign policy bureaucracy has less of an impact on the making or implementing of policy.[46]

The end of the Cold War, the spread of liberal economic restructuring, and redemocratization have turned Chile into an "ordinary" country for many political forces in the United States. This has lowered the profile of Chile in U.S. policy and has made foreign policy more routinized and bureaucratic. Reduced priority in U.S. foreign policy has advantages and disadvantages for a country, which we will examine in more detail in subsequent chapters.

The foreign policy process has also been altered on the Chilean side where redemocratization has opened up the process to both congressional scrutiny and public lobbying. The Chilean government is thus more domestically constrained in its relations with the United States. Once again, the change in the process in itself does not determine whether the bilateral relationship will improve or deteriorate.

Diplomatic Relations

One of the international consequences of the military coup of 1973 had been Chile's ostracism from the chief international fora. The new democratic government of Patricio Aylwin (1990–1994) embarked upon diplomatic incentives that were successful enough in the first year to recover Chile's historical international presence.

Relations with the United States began to normalize and become cooperative with the return of democracy to Chile. President Aylwin became the first Chilean president since 1962 to travel to the United States, and President Bush quickly reciprocated in December 1990. That end-of-the-year meeting produced agreements that resolved some of the outstanding problems in the relationship (see Chapter Five).

Progress continued during the Frei administration (1994–2000) when bilateral relations became more institutionalized. In Frei's first year, a Political Consultation System was developed to encourage dialogue on contentious issues, discover opportunities for cooperation, and coordinate policies. Frei's trip to Washington in March 1997 marked an important moment in the bilateral relationship when the Chilean leader told the U.S. Congress:

> My presence here symbolizes a new era in friendship with the people of the United States. We want to leave fears and distrust behind. We know that we live in a precious time, an opportunity we cannot lose. A time between two

historical processes. We are neither an economic nor a military power but we want to be a part of the history that is being born. Allies in the solution of the most pressing problems that confront us all. Partners in furthering freedom. Brothers in the promotion of peace and democracy.[47]

President Clinton was no less eloquent in his speech before the Chilean Congress in 1998:

> The twenty-first century will be the century of democracy. To those who in whatever part of the Americas would try to take away the people's precious liberties once again, or would seek to govern again through terror and violence, we repeat the historic words of President Aylwin in Santiago stadium, "Never again."... We are your largest trading partner and trade between us has grown an average of thirteen percent per year since 1993. We want and will resolutely pursue a free trade agreement that includes our two nations and we will not be satisfied until we have achieved that objective. Chile and the United States should be full partners in the twenty-first century. We should also fully associate ourselves with the democracies of our region with similar aspirations.[48]

At the official dinner for President Clinton, President Frei developed Clinton's goal of being full partners by pointing to the shared problems of the two nations, subtly suggesting that the United States too faces the problems posed by inequality of wealth:

> These are times of promise, but also times of challenge. In an earlier era, we could contrast the wealthy world of the North with the impoverished South. Today we find rich and poor in all countries, and it seems that the mechanisms of social exclusion have also become global. In many more countries than we may think, wide inequalities persist between men and women; serious deficiencies remain in education, housing, health, and access to dignified work; and drug addiction and violence are presented as escape routes in the face of expectations which do not correspond to reality. I believe, Mr. President, that we share many of these concerns, and for that reason, relations between your country and mine have better prospects than ever before in history.[49]

In addition to his state visit, Clinton's most important personal diplomacy for the bilateral relationship came at the Second Summit of the Americas. In his inaugural speech he implicitly accepted Fei's point that governments must address the issues of inequality that are heightened by the opportunities of the new economy:

> The Miami Summit was the decisive moment in the history of our hemisphere because the leaders of free peoples adopted a common vision for the future and a common strategy to reach it. Poverty throughout the

> hemisphere is far too high, civil society is far too fragile, justice systems too weak, too many people lack education and the necessary skills to triumph in the new economy. In short, too few people feel that the changes are working for them.[50]

Despite the great differences in foreign policy between the military and democratic governments, certain continuities persist. These continuities revolve around four principal elements that provide the guidelines under which Chile addresses disputes with neighbors, organizes deterrence, and institutionalizes its international linkages. The four elements are Americanism, political nationalism, the rule of law, and alignment with Western civilization.

Americanism builds on what was called the Western Hemisphere ideal in the nineteenth century[51] when political processes and national interests were defined in contrast to the power politics and antidemocratic polities of Europe. In the twentieth century these sentiments create regional solidarity. While of great importance during the Cold War, in the contemporary period they signify the possibility of organizing hemispheric relations around the ideals of democracy and extensive free trade.

Political nationalism reflects the strong national identity that Chile projects in its foreign policy, bringing a distinctly Chilean perspective to its international relations. The principal manifestations arise around the concepts of autonomy and self-determination. The historical primacy of this distinctive Chilean identity may be one of the elements of Chilean foreign policy that will undergo the most change in the post–Cold War period as a result of the process of globalization.

Rule of law and consequent search for an international regime enshrining it is a third component of Chile's traditional foreign policy. Given the size of the country, its chief resources lie not in the use of force, but in the acceptance of the principles of juridical equality and the establishment of an international system that respects identity and national sovereignty. It is within this context that the sanctity of treaties plays a fundamental role.

Alignment with the West, the fourth key element of Chilean foreign policy, was automatic during the Cold War. Even under the Allende government, Chile sought merely to universalize its international linkages, not shift its international alignments. In this bipolar period, Chile's civilian governments perceived alignment as privileging international peace and cooperation above ideological boundaries as the fundamental issues. They believed that international peace builds on a foundation of cooperation and confrontation of ideas, not the clash of ideologies and of violent conflict. Today this alignment with the West is expressed via support for democracy and human rights as guiding principles of international life.[52]

Military Relations

The military relationship has also changed, and for the better. This relationship remained problematic even after the transition to democracy, largely because of the Kennedy embargo. Smaller irritants were the continued political role of General Pinochet after the transition and the new government's willingness to continue a military modernization policy that upgraded weapons systems beyond those the United States desired for Latin America.

1991 marked the turning point for military relations, with repeal of the Kennedy legislation that banned arms sales to Chile and the Washington visit of Chile's civilian minister of defense, Patricio Rojas. During this visit an agreement was signed providing Chile with: 1) participation in the Foreign Military Sales system; 2) participation in military training and education programs in U.S. military education institutions; 3) an agreement to further explore joint maneuvers between the respective navies, air forces, and armies; and 4) the possibility of linking Chilean military hospitals, public universities, and the Ministry of Health with the data banks of the National Medical Library in the United States.

The Chilean Navy, Army, and Air Force began joint exercises with U. S. military units that same year. The military exercises, "Joint Forces—Chile 91" and "Operation UNITAS XXXII," took place in northern Chile between June 30 and July 13. The Chilean Army supervised the exercises with participants from the Chilean Navy, Air Force, and approximately 110 people from the Southern Command of the U.S. Army.

These were followed by more joint activities in June of 1992. Specialists at the Defense Resource Management Institute in Monterey, California, held a seminar in which forty-eight officials from the armed forces and civilians worked on decision-making processes. The seminar included topics such as planning, programming, utilization of national resources, cost-benefit analysis, as well as decision-analysis and simulation exercises.

The two Concertación governments since redemocratization have been interested in making Chilean defense policy less suspicious to its neighbors. They also want to use defense policy to reduce the military's involvement in politics by focusing on professionalization issues. In pursuit of these goals, the two governments embarked on regional policies designed to build confidence with Chile's past rivals, Argentina and Peru. One particularly important policy was the development of a Defense White Paper that outlined national defense rationales and policies. The U.S. government was also pursuing confidence-building measures in the hemisphere and saw defense white papers as an integral part of the new structure of hemispheric security relations. Consequently, when Chile became the first Latin American government to publish a Defense White Paper it coincided well with U.S. policy and made Chile and the United States partners in convincing others to follow suit.

These confidence-building measures also served Chile and the United States well when it came time to renovate Chile's warplanes. In 1997 the Clinton administration decided to accept its lack of control over arms sales to the region and overturned a twenty-year ban on the sale of sophisticated U.S. weapons to Latin

America.[53] Chile benefits by being able to consider the U.S. F-16 plane and the U.S. arms industry may make another sale. Under the new regional context of peace, however, these possibilities have not provoked an arms race.

A major change in the relationship would have been stimulated by Chile's incorporation into the North American Free Trade Association (NAFTA) among Canada, Mexico, and the United States. Chilean advocates of joining NAFTA were more interested in the signal such a partnership would send to the international community rather than in the specific trade benefits it would generate. These were likely to be small, given the limited trade between Chile and the United States, the participation of Chile in the U.S. Generalized System of Preferences (GSP) program, and the existence of free trade agreements with Mexico and Canada independent of NAFTA. While the structural economic relationship might not have changed much, the bureaucratic form of that relationship would have become more institutionalized, as the NAFTA bureaucracy comprises multiple working groups and annual presidential summits.

The Impact of the End of the Cold War

The two-year period of 1988 and 1989 represents a watershed for the relationship between Chile and the United States. Around the world everyone will remember this as a time when the Iron Curtain was breached, leading ultimately to the fall of the Berlin Wall and the disappearance of the German Democratic Republic. But the end of the Cold War was a secondary event for Chileans. 1988 will be forever etched in Chile's history as the year in which General Pinochet lost a plebiscite for an extension of his rule for another eight years. The presidential elections that ushered in the transition to democracy took place the following year.

The end of the Cold War had a segmented impact on Chilean political behavior. For the 43 percent of Chile's electorate that supported Pinochet, perestroika and the collapse of communism in central Europe did not alleviate fears generated by the specter of a transition to democracy. This large fraction of Chileans worried then, and still today, that democracy would hearken a return to socialist influence in Chile's polity and, along with it, renewed strife as in the Allende years. In the eyes of the Chilean right, the collapse of the Soviet Union was less important than the viability of the Chilean left.

Within the Chilean left, the collapse of communism strengthened the influence of those with social-democratic tendencies (known as *renovados* in the Chilean Socialist Party). The transition to democracy owes a great deal to the willingness of these members of the left to work within the institutional rules that set up (and make difficult to alter) "authoritarian enclaves" in Chile's political system.[54] (For a discussion, see Chapter Three.)

The end of the Cold War was undoubtedly one of the major events in U.S. history. But the fall of communism played only a partial and indirect role in the U.S. response to Chile's efforts to redemocratize and in the bilateral relationship in general. While the United States has always supported democracy *per se*, its Cold War strategy had traditionally subordinated such support to the need to prevent "Communists" from achieving power, even through the ballot box.[55] Internal factors in U.S. domestic politics and external events helped push support for democracy to equal status with fighting communism by the mid-1980s.

The election of Ronald Reagan in 1980 brought forth a new era of ideological politics. At first this was expressed in a renewed emphasis on combating communism, even with the support of authoritarian governments.[56] Domestic opposition to the Reagan administration's Contra offensive against the Sandinista government in Nicaragua, however, helped propel U.S. policy into supporting democracy as a goal in itself.

External events also helped produce the shift in U.S. foreign policy. The Gorbachev reforms in the Soviet Union and subsequently the peaceful ouster of communist governments in the former Warsaw Pact nations made it more likely that the United States would continue to support democracy even if those political forces traditionally friendly to the United States did not win. The new wave of redemocratization in Latin America in the 1980s made it difficult for the United States to change course even with a new administration. George Bush justified his conflictual policies in 1988 and 1989 with a previous ally in Panama partly by focusing on General Manuel Noriega's antidemocratic character.

The end of the Cold War facilitated a shift in U.S. foreign policy goals, but the country and government were already moving to promote democratization and free trade throughout the hemisphere. The basis for a change in U.S. foreign policy that would move the two countries closer together after 1989 was thus already in place by the time communism collapsed in Europe.

Conclusion

Chile and the United States had initial advantages vis-à-vis their neighbors that provided for early domination of their immediate neighborhoods. Chile and the United States began their relationship by competing for regional dominance, and the United States was cautious not to challenge Chile openly at this time. Chile confronted the geopolitical and economic limits to its expansion just as the United States was becoming more active in South America. Competition remained the norm, but because Chile's policy-makers and political elite recognized the wisdom of becoming a status quo power, that competition was never pushed to the breaking point.

World War II ended with the destruction of all of the great power rivals to the United States save one, the USSR. Within Chile, the governments of 1948 to 1964 moved against the Communist Party for domestic reasons. Under these international and domestic conditions, Chile and the United States found much in common. Yet these same conditions of international bipolarity and U.S. anticommunism meant that when Chilean politics moved first leftward in 1970, then fiercely rightward in 1973, the implications for the bilateral relationship would be profoundly negative.

The dramatic changes that occurred in Chile in 1990 and within the international system in the 1980s provided a context for renewing the Chile-U.S. relationship. Cooperation was not a foregone conclusion because many important issues remained to be negotiated or accommodated. Yet the combination of redemocratization and the end of bipolarity would make it possible for the United States and Chile to discover common interests and increasingly engage in cooperative ventures after 1990.

FOREIGN POLICY DECISION-MAKING IN THE RELATIONSHIP

TWO

INTERNATIONAL FACTORS IN THE CHILEAN-U.S. RELATIONSHIP

BILATERAL RELATIONS TAKE PLACE WITHIN AN INTERNATIONAL context. Consequently, the characteristics of that context will affect the bilateral relationship. It is fruitful to conceive of the impact of the international system upon nations as occurring chiefly through two mechanisms. Alterations in the international system affect the *creation and elimination of opportunities* for states at the international level. Those opportunities, in turn, affect the *distribution of political influence among domestic socioeconomic groups* vying for national policy influence. In this chapter we will focus on the former mechanism by which international factors affect the U.S.-Chilean bilateral relationship, leaving the latter for examination in the next chapter.

A bilateral relationship reflects how much each side needs the other and the priority a partner is willing to give the relationship in its general international politics. Of particular interest in studying Chilean U.S. relations is the increased level of cooperation in the contemporary period. Cooperation is defined as the mutual adjustment of policy. Since all adjustments require movement away from a state's ideal policy, states cooperate only when acting unilaterally does not appear to be advantageous.[1] Some changes at the international level make cooperative efforts among states more likely, while other changes create new opportunities for taking unilateral action.

In this chapter we examine the creation of new international opportunities for Chile and the United States, as well as the policy responses of each country that were characterized by a broad domestic policy consensus. Such policies clearly represent the national interest and can be expected to continue despite alterations of personalities and parties in power. In Spanish they are known as "políticas de estado"; in English the phrase "national interest" comes closest to conveying its meaning.

Four major points contribute to understanding the international impact on contemporary Chile-U.S. relations. First, an international normative order has been created that emphasizes democracy and markets. Although it functions imperfectly, Chile must comply with this normative order if it wishes to take advantage of international opportunities. Second, the development of unipolarity implies that balancing strategies are less attractive for small countries like Chile than climbing on the U.S. bandwagon. Third, because the United States is the unipolar power, it is likely to be preoccupied elsewhere; thus Chile will find it advantageous to develop and implement active international "self-help" strategies that are complementary to its position on the bandwagon. Fourth, and another consequence of U.S. unipolarity, small countries like Chile will attempt to ensnare the United States within international institutions as the most likely way to constrain U.S. interventionism and unilateralism.

This chapter first examines systemic changes in the international political-military sphere and in the international economy. Subsequently we focus on regime change in the policy arenas of most concern to Chile. The concluding section summarizes the contributions of international factors to the bilateral relationship and uses their limitations to point the way to discussions in subsequent chapters of the importance of domestic and transnational factors.

Systemic Changes in the International Arena

The International Political-Military Sphere

Three systemic changes in the post–Cold War period stand out as fundamentally important for understanding U.S.-Chilean relations in the 1990s. These are the development of unipolarity, the redefinition of security, and the modification of concepts of sovereignty.

The end of the Cold War produced changes in the framework that organized geographic zones of influence and the way in which disputes among and within states were addressed. For half a century, Cold War strategic themes dominated the agenda, with international security defined by the bipolar confrontation despite attempts by many developing countries to remain outside bipolar competition. Today proxy wars stimulated or aggravated by superpowers no longer pose a threat to international security. Yet interstate wars have not ceased, and NATO is more active today than ever.

The context within which war occurs has changed. Today the international system is unipolar. The international implications of the United States using military force, alone or with its military alliance NATO, are fundamentally different. Global war is highly unlikely, and no nation can deter the remaining great power. Consequently, the use of force to support the great power's international agenda is increasingly likely.

The development of unipolarity also affected the relative importance of small countries. When the competition between the two great powers was global, they tended to see every country as important to the overall balance of power.[2] For good or ill, these states attracted the attention of the United States and the USSR. Now, however, the value of states is less strategic and more economic and moral. Attractiveness on economic criteria can bring resources for development. Moral criteria, however, mainly provide the negative incentive of drawing sanctions onto a government perceived by the United States and Europe to be violating certain international norms regarding human rights and, to a lesser degree, democracy.

TABLE 2.1

Use of Force in the Western Hemisphere after the End of the Cold War

Year	Dyad	Hostility Level[a]
1990	None	
1991	Honduras/Nicaragua	4
	Peru/Ecuador	3
	U.S.-OAS/Haiti	3
1992	U.S.-OAS/Haiti	4
1993	U.S.-OAS/Haiti	4
1994	U.S./Haiti	4
	Ecuador/Peru	2
1995	Ecuador/Peru	5
	Ecuador/Peru	4
	Colombia/Venezuela	4
	Nicaragua/Honduras	4
	Nicaragua/Colombia	2
1996	Nicaragua/Honduras	4
	Nicaragua/El Salvador	4
	Honduras/El Salvador	4
1997	Honduras/Nicaragua	4
	Nicaragua/Costa Rica	3
	El Salvador/Honduras	3
	Venezuela/Colombia	4
	Belize/Guatemala	4
1998	Ecuador/Peru	3
	Costa Rica/Nicaragua	3
	Nicaragua/Honduras	3
1999	Nicaragua/Honduras	3

[a] Hostility levels: 1 = no use; 2 = threat; 3 = display; 4 = use < 1,000 battlefield-related deaths; 5 = war.

Sources: Militarized Interstate Dispute database, revised version, to 1992; *Keesing's Contemporary Archives*; *ChipNews/Santiago Times* (Santiago, Chile); *NotiSur* and *EcoCentral*; *Hoy* (Quito, Ecuador); and *La Nación* (San José, Costa Rica).

The diminished importance of small state conflict to the remaining superpower means that the security threats small countries face may not be the same as those identified by the leader of the system. In the specific case of Latin America, interstate conflicts among Latin American countries were not primarily the product of the Cold War. Rather they reflected local power relations, border disagreements, and the uncontrolled movement of people. Hence the end of the Cold War did not mean that the security context of small states ceased to be of concern to them. In the Western Hemisphere, traditional security concerns continued to produce the use of force in interstate affairs, as indicated in Table 2.1.

With the end of superpower confrontation, the fear of nuclear war subsided and was replaced by a fear of conventional war among states on the periphery.[3]

Yet the possibility remains that minor nuclear powers may confront one another. Despite publicized nuclear tests designed to strengthen deterrence, India and Pakistan escalated their territorial dispute in 1999 into serious artillery exchanges and air strikes. Thus the specter of nuclear proliferation and nuclear war remains alive, even if only at a regional level.

The end of the Cold War also brought to the forefront of international politics questions related to transnational forces and national political processes. The themes of international security in the last decade now range from domestic human rights issues, to the defense of political democracy, to environmental degradation. This expansion of the concept of security means that the domain of sovereignty, at least for the smaller powers, is diminished.

The manner in which problems are confronted or force used has also changed. The international political-military context immediately after the Cold War was characterized by much enthusiasm for mechanisms to prevent and resolve conflicts at the regional level. Building on the European experience, and to a lesser extent on the Tlatelolco proscription of nuclear weapons in Latin America, arms control and confidence-building measures became increasingly popular mechanisms around the globe.

At the same time, multilateral intervention, including the use of military force, to stop or resolve conflicts has become legitimate. Between 1945 and 1990, the UN imposed sanctions on a country twice; in 1991 alone it imposed four sanctions. From 1945 to 1985 the UN engaged in thirteen peacekeeping missions; in 1994 it was involved in 18.[4] While most of the international interventions have been led by the United States, Nigeria has also put together an intervention force in West Africa.

Impact on the United States

The systemic changes at the political-military level produced by the end of the Cold War had a fundamental impact on U.S. foreign policy. As the unipolar power, the United States could reorganize much of the system to reflect U.S. values and strengths. The political values promoted by the United States were liberal democracy, liberal markets, and a liberal conception of human rights, except on the death penalty.[5] Because the U.S. economy went through a painful restructuring process in the 1980s, it was also poised to take advantage of the accelerating globalization process in the 1990s.

As the only remaining superpower, the United States is in the enviable position of possessing great freedom of action, at least in the short run. If the United States uses that freedom poorly, however, it will confront serious challenges in the international arena from two sources. When confronting problems that can be resolved only via cooperative efforts with other nations, unilateral action may mitigate some problems in the short term, but the problems will recur, perhaps in more severe form. In addition, too much unilateral action will likely produce resentments and fears among other states, thereby stimulating efforts by other nations to diminish their vulnerability to the United States.

This new international context affected other states in a manner that was beneficial to the United States. During the Cold War, some statesmen and social groups sought a middle ground between the superpowers. In the 1990s there was no middle ground, and one side had clearly "won." Consequently, statesmen and social groups sought to curry favor with the United States, thereby effectively conferring upon its view a great deal of influence over their own policy preferences.

In the Western Hemisphere, this special attraction articulated itself as the "Washington Consensus" concerning liberal markets and democratic governments. The first Summit of the Americas was held in Miami in 1994 and included all the democratically elected presidents of the hemisphere. A subsequent summit was held in Santiago de Chile (April 1998). Since 1995, presidential summits have been complemented by periodic meetings of defense ministers (1995 in Williamsburg, United States; 1996 in Bariloche, Argentina; 1998 in Cartagena, Colombia). Each of the summits is designed to stimulate action on the components of the "Washington Consensus."

During the Cold War, the United States utilized its military force in the name of containing Soviet expansion and aggression. A decade after the end of the Cold War, however, the United States continues to maintain over two hundred military bases in thirty-five countries and possessions around the globe.[6] Despite concern by the post-Soviet Russian government, the United States expanded its military alliance eastward in Europe to incorporate the major military allies of its old rival (Poland, the Czech Republic, and Hungary, along with the former German Democratic Republic, which had been reunited with the German Federal Republic).

It is ironic that many analysts had believed that United States intervention was stimulated by the competition between the United States and Soviet Union. Today the United States uses its military force for almost everything except to defend the United States against a military attack. In no other ten-year period of U.S. history has military force been used in so many different places (see Table 2.2). With hindsight we might better say that bipolarity limited U.S. military adventurism. In the new age of unipolarity, no one has been able to stop the United States for long.

Although the United States will not always use force, it has demonstrated a significant willingness to utilize its military might in support of its international goals. Nevertheless, the United States confronts a tension between its historic tendency toward isolation and a desire to be the leader, if not policeman, of the world. International factors push the United States toward playing an active role. Yet we need only remember U.S. isolationism between 1933 and 1941, while the world drifted into world war, to recognize that domestic factors may override international "imperatives."

TABLE 2.2

Use of Military Force by the United States 1989–1999

Year	Place	Type of Operation	Official Justification
1989	Panama	Invasion	Stop drug trafficking/promote democracy; defend U.S. lives
1990–1991	Persian Gulf	War	Coerce Iraqi to retreat/deter future aggression
1991–1994	Haiti	Embargo, threats, show of force; invasion avoided at last minute	Defend human rights and democracy/stop migration
1993	Iraq	Show of force; punishment	Coerce Iraq on arms inspections/no-fly zone
1993–1994	Somalia	Peacekeeping	Defend human rights
1994–1995	Bosnia	Military coercion; peacekeeping	Defend human rights
1996	Taiwan Straits	Show of force	Deter China
1998	Afghanistan/ Sudan	Punishment	Fight terrorism
1998	Iraq	Punishment	Coerce Iraq on arms inspections
1999	Kosovo	Military coercion; peacekeeping	Defend human rights/deter aggression
2000	Iraq	Punishment	Coerce Iraq on no-fly zone

Despite its status as the unipolar power and its demonstrated willingness to use force, the United States cannot control the behavior of other states, even in the Western Hemisphere. The efficiency of U.S. foreign policy is enhanced if others share similar goals and agree to pursue them in similar ways. The United States therefore tries to help structure a context in which other states will find it to be in their own interests to behave in ways compatible with U.S. interests. Although this effort has been most successful in the economic arena, progress is developing on security issues as well.

Since the 1980s various Latin American nations have emphasized peaceful resolution of conflict and confidence-building between historic rivals.[7] Regional meetings on mutual confidence-building measures were held under the auspices of the OAS in Santiago in 1995 and in San Salvador in 1998. Progress on mutual confidence-building measures reinforces a long-standing U.S. sentiment that the armed forces in Latin America really had nothing to do except undermine democracy. This attitude led the United States to replace national armies with national guards when it was directly intervening in most Caribbean countries in the 1920s.

Although for political reasons it cannot be official U.S. policy, many policy-makers in Washington looked with favor upon the Haitian and Panamanian decisions to disband their militaries in the early 1990s.

As peaceful resolution of conflict and confidence-building progresses in the region, the United States must confront the question: What should be done with the militaries that continue to exist? The United States favors coastal defense missions and participation in international peacekeeping, as well as a major role in drug eradication and interdiction. The Clinton administration, nevertheless, adopted some policies that send a different message, such as conferring "major non-NATO ally" status upon Argentina and agreeing to sell sophisticated arms in the region after a twenty-year hiatus. These policies work to the advantage of advocates for militaries the size and sophistication of those in Brazil, Chile, or Peru.

The collapse of its only political and military challenger (the Soviet Union) means that the United States does not have to worry about a rival in the region. No country other than the United States is interested in having military access to the region. Everyone is free to sell conventional weapons in the region, and Europe and Japan can invest and trade in the hemisphere without provoking U.S. security concerns and countermeasures (as occurred during the early twentieth century). This new situation allows the United States to focus on other issues in the hemisphere, thereby helping to mitigate Latin American fears of U.S. security policy (though the militarization of U.S. drug policy worries many Latin American nations).

Impact on Chile

Chile was also fundamentally affected by the structural changes in the international political-military sphere. Because of its international position as a small power, Chile confronted a number of opportunities and constraints different from those affecting the United States.

In the area of security, Chile continues to confront some challenges. Bolivia still desires a sovereign outlet to the Pacific Ocean, which it lost to Chile in the War of the Pacific (1879–1884). The country does not have diplomatic relations with Chile at the ambassadorial level, and the current democratically elected Bolivian president, Hugo Banzer, has publicly called for Chile to negotiate a Bolivian outlet to the sea. Bolivia also denounced Chilean mines at the Land Mine Conference in Canada.[8]

Chile and Argentina almost went to war in 1978, and Chile aided Great Britain against Argentina in the Malvinas/Falklands War of 1982. Under President Carlos Saul Menem (1990–2000) Argentina adopted the new vision of peaceful hemispheric relations, and the final border disagreements with Chile were peacefully resolved in 1999. Yet Argentine political history cautions prudence while waiting to see if Menem's successors will continue to be favorably disposed to good relations with Chile.

Security relations with Peru, with which Chile had a war scare in 1974 to 1976, have also improved. All disagreements over the 1929 peace accord were resolved in 1999. The respective visits of Presidents Fujimori and Frei demonstrated that the countries are on the verge of a new stage in their relations as the twenty-first century begins.[9] To the degree that confidence on security matters depends heavily upon democracy, however, the aftermath of Fujimori's resignation and flight to Japan in 2000 may undermine Chilean confidence in Peru.

Chile has developed a strategic doctrine that privileges defensive deterrence. Chile looks at the strategic and not merely military balance of power. The strategic balance takes into consideration a country's political, economic, military, and diplomatic assets.[10] Of particular importance in developing a favorable strategic balance are confidence-building measures that nurture trust among neighbors, attract the interest of third parties, and free up resources for political and economic development. Military policy thus complements twentieth-century Chilean traditions privileging diplomacy and international law, based upon recognition of and a respect for treaties and accords. In line with this strategic doctrine, Chile developed the first Defense White Paper in the region; Argentina followed suit in 1999. Consequently, Chile has developed a common interest with the United States in persuading other South American nations to produce their own defense white papers.

Chile's military doctrine is defense-oriented, despite the country's lack of strategic depth. The goal is to communicate to a potential aggressor that it cannot be assured of winning control of major assets and would pay a high price for any attempt at aggression. This Chilean policy benefits from changes in the arms market that have increased competition as arms suppliers that had previously been devoted to the Cold War conflict look for new clients. Chile has had the will and funds to purchase in this market[11] and may become the first client for F-16 fighters under the new U.S. policy.[12] Chilean and U.S. cooperation in this arena is thus based on Chilean interest in buying more sophisticated weapons and U.S. interest in selling them.

The government developed its policy on peacekeeping operations in November 1996. Chile reserves the right to examine each peacekeeping situation on a case-by-case basis and will not participate in any efforts to impose peace. The missions in which Chile will participate require a clear mandate for action from the United Nations. Chilean personnel will be civilian or military professionals, preferably volunteers. Under no circumstances will conscripts be deployed.[13] Minister of Foreign Affairs Soledad Alvear has indicated that playing a role in defending international peace is "an ethical imperative, because it reflects the aspirations of humanity, and secondly because a peaceful world is beneficial for development and the well-being of its peoples."[14] Among the specific benefits generated by this participation are an improvement in the inter-operational abilities of the Chilean armed forces, and the international demonstration of the professional capacities of the Chilean Armed Forces. (Table 2.3.)

TABLE 2.3

Chilean Participation in Peacekeeping Operations

Operation	Dates	Location	Form of Participation
Outside the Western Hemisphere			
UNMOGIP	1949-present	India/Pakistan	3 army officials
UNTSO	1967-present	Palestine	3 armed forces officials
UNIKOM	1991–1992	Iraq/Kuwait	Air force helicopter unit
UNTAC	1992–1993	Cambodia	Navy
UNSCOM	1996–1998	Iraq	41 air force personnel and 5 helicopters
UNTAET	1999-present	East Timor	Army personnel
UNIPTF	1997-present	Bosnia-Herzegovina	Carabineros personnel
Within the Western Hemisphere			
OAS	1969	Honduras/El Salvador	Military observers
ONUSAL	1991–1992	El Salvador	Carabineros personnel
OAS	1993	Nicaragua	De-mining specialists
MOMEP	1995–1998	Ecuador-Peru	Military observers
MINUGUA	1996-present	Guatemala	Police and investigations personnel

The Chilean government deplored the military intervention in Kosovo. An official communique noted that Chile "deplores that the need for an authorization of the Security Council of the United Nations—organization responsible for international peace and security—has been ignored. Because of this, Chile expresses its concern over the decision to use force as a means to resolve the crisis in which Kosovo lives and emphasizes the urgent need to implement resolution 1160 (1998) of the Council addressing this conflict." The government of Chile demanded the immediate interruption of the bombing of Yugoslavia and at the same time called upon the Yugoslav authorities and Albanian leaders of Kosovo to reconvene at the earliest moment the dialogue that would facilitate the quick reestablishment of peace in the region. It was hoped that the talks would respect the sovereignty and territorial integrity of the parties as well as the legitimate rights of ethnic minorities.[15]

Chief among the challenges for Chilean political-military policy is to participate in the new sense of security cooperation and confidence-building with the appropriate balance between optimism and prudence. Too optimistic a foreign policy might significantly increase Chile's vulnerability if these changes prove to be merely reflective of this transitional stage in international politics. Yet adopting a policy that errs on the side of prudence could contribute to the closing up of these new opportunities for cooperation and stability.

Globalization of the World Economy

The term "globalization" is best used to describe the development of a worldwide capital market, the internationalization of the production process, and significantly increased levels of trade. It refers not simply to the fact of interaction, for capital and goods have flowed around the world since the days of European colonialism. Instead globalization reflects the magnitude of that interaction and the tremendous speed at which that interaction occurs. Globalization in this sense represents a major change in the structure of the international economy; it reached a new phase when the end of the Cold War opened up major markets in the world to international capital.

The origins of globalization can be laid at the doorstep of the Bretton Woods system, especially the General Agreement on Tariffs and Trade (GATT, created in 1947), and the development of the Eurodollar market in the 1960s. The GATT lowered barriers to trade in manufactured products and established the principle of liberalizing trade as long as it was politically feasible in the advanced industrialized countries.[16] The Eurodollar market burst onto the international scene in the 1960s, producing an important expansion of liquidity in the international system that fueled increases in world trade.[17]

The recycling of petrodollars after 1973 further stimulated a greater integration of Third World economies with the economies of advanced industrialized societies.[18] The dramatic increase in the price of oil produced a major transfer of capital from the advanced industrialized countries (rich consumers of large amounts of petroleum products) to the oil-producing countries (mainly sparsely populated Arab sheikdoms or less-developed countries). Some of these countries could not spend all they earned, while others had needs that exceeded this windfall. The international banks offered a means of investing excess funds or borrowing on future profits. As a result, the banks moved enormous sums of money around the world, effectively tying national economies together in new and volatile ways.

The international debt crisis of the 1980s can be seen, with hindsight, as the growing pains of this process. The magnitude of the crisis was possible only because of globalization, and its resolution provided new ways for capital to flow through the system and tie economies more firmly together. Although the debt crisis has not been solved,[19] and the mobility of capital continues to threaten developing countries,[20] the alternatives to participating in globalization remain distinctly worse.

Globalization has stimulated greater efforts for economic integration at the regional or subregional level as well. The Europeans further consolidated the Common Market into the European Union and expanded its membership. In Asia, the Asia-Pacific Economic Cooperation forum (APEC) brought the Asian nations together with Australia, the United States, Canada, and even some Latin American countries to discuss common concerns. Within Latin America there have been multiple efforts at subregional integration: the Group of Three (Mexico, Colombia, and

Venezuela), the Central American Integration System, the Andean Pact, and Mercosur.[21] Numerous bilateral pacts have also been signed, with Chile as the principal country making these kinds of ties in Latin America. And Mercosur is attempting to develop cross-regionally by attaining a special relationship with the EU.

Globalization has produced an international political-economic context that punishes states seeking to develop via insulation of their national economies from international competition. Hence import-substitution industrialization (ISI) schemes reached a dead end in places like Latin America that had already completed the "easy" phases of ISI. Private foreign investment and the International Monetary Fund (IMF) had been used in conjunction with stabilization policies to overcome foreign exchange bottlenecks that developed as ISI moved into more capital-intensive phases. But the development of a global capital market and the opening of national markets to more foreign trade called for structural adjustment of the economies, not stabilization.

In this new international context, marginalization is the chief external threat for Latin America. Leaders in the hemisphere have attempted to integrate their economies in response to this challenge. Unlike the efforts of the 1950s to 1970s, however, this time the integration is more pragmatic than ideological and oriented toward integrating into rather than isolating Latin American markets from the global economy.[22] The structural reforms of varying degrees implemented by Latin American countries as a result of the debt crisis have also made it easier to integrate their economies.

The most success has been at the subregional and bilateral levels. Governmental agreements have led private actors to produce practical effects in business, investment, exchanges, commerce, transport, and tourism. Agreements among private actors, in turn, stimulate a greater demand for agreements among governments.

Impact of Globalization on the United States

The United States was initially challenged by these changes, as high inflation and low growth in the 1970s seemed to foretell the weakening of the U.S. industrial sector. Japanese ascendancy seemed assured, and U.S. foreign economic policy became defensive in the Trade Acts of 1974 and 1979.[23]

Ronald Reagan was elected president in 1980 on a platform that denied that the U.S. economy had reached its structural limits. Government regulation was deemed to be the culprit. The transition to a new motor (information rather than industry) for the economy was costly, and the government generated huge deficits to fund it (as well as to pay for a massive military buildup). As of 1999, the strategy appears to have been phenomenally successful, as the economy has experienced the longest period of economic growth with low inflation in the post–Cold War period. And unlike the European and Latin American recoveries in the 1990s, the United States accomplished this while driving unemployment rates to their lowest rates in three decades.

The United States was not just focused on the recovery of its own economy. It played a major role in developing a new strategy for debt management in the 1980s. The U.S. Treasury had always been a safety net beneath the IMF, but it was not called upon in a major way until the level of international debt, stimulated by the increased liquidity in the system, overwhelmed the resources of the IMF. The United States first aided Mexico with its debt in 1982 (and would do so again in 1994) and then put pressure upon U.S. banks to restructure their international loans in a manner that would avoid defaults on private sector debt. The United States also worked with other major lending countries to restructure official debt. And the United States began to pressure the IMF to move away from a focus on stabilization of balance of payments to an emphasis on structural adjustment within the economies in crisis.

Given the magnitude of the international debt crisis, these efforts were not sufficient to bring the crisis under control for at least the medium term. The U.S. Treasury thus took a more direct role in March 1982 under Secretary Nicholas Brady. Brady was responding to the failure of his predecessor Howard Baker's efforts at restoring growth and development in debtor countries. The new policy continued to insist on the importance of economic policy reform in debtor countries. Unlike the Baker Plan's emphasis on the need to maintain debt payments, the Brady Plan focused on creating new instruments for accelerating debt reduction. For example, prorating clauses and negative guarantees included in debt contracts were suspended for three years. These clauses required that debtors obtain approval from private banks before converting debts into long-term bonds. The plan also called on lending governments to explore methods of modifying bank regulations in order to reduce debts of developing countries. Eliminating these clauses and altering banking regulations created an environment in which governments of debtor countries could reach ad hoc agreements with banks for reducing debts. The U.S. government also committed itself to increased support of the International Monetary Fund while insisting that the IMF and the World Bank allocate funds specifically to support debt reduction.[24]

The U.S. domestic experience of the 1980s became the model that the United States expected others to follow. At first, the "Washington Consensus" referred to the economic policy instruments perceived necessary to generate renewed growth in Latin America. These instruments were designed to provide macroeconomic prudence, outward orientation, and domestic liberalization.[25] Policies were to establish fiscal discipline, prioritize education and health for public spending, implement tax reform, allow the market to determine interest and exchange rates, liberalize trade policies, promote greater openness toward foreign investment, privatize public enterprises, deregulate the economy, and protect private property. Democracy was later added to the "Washington Consensus" as the only political system that was acceptable in the hemisphere.

The terms of the consensus reflected an agreement among U.S. academics, economic consultants, and officials from the U.S. government, IMF, and World Bank reached during a 1989 meeting in Washington. The consensus was not a consensus of the international community arrived at after a broad debate concerning the needs and options confronting the world as it approached the twenty-first century.

Regional trade pacts were another means of strengthening the U.S. economy in the face of increased international competition. The United States began with a Free Trade Agreement with Canada in 1988, which subsequently developed into the North American Free Trade Agreement (NAFTA) and included Mexico in 1994. The Caribbean Basin Initiative (CBI) provided trade incentives for small countries in the Caribbean and Central America to trade with the United States. When Mexico joined NAFTA, however, many of the CBI advantages were undercut.

President Bush announced on June 27, 1990, an "Enterprise Initiative for the Americas." This policy was to be the centerpiece of a new relationship with Latin America and covered trade, investment, and debt.[26] The initiative was envisioned to be a medium-term project, proceeding by steps. The United States proposed that framework agreements be established to promote trade liberalization while preliminary discussions were carried out in an official forum. The United States also encouraged Latin American countries to work together in subregional groupings on lowering barriers to trade. A multilateral fund financed by the major industrialized countries to help countries develop investment policies to attract private foreign investment was promised but never created. The debt issue in the region was to be addressed by the Brady Plan and debt-for-nature swaps (with a side benefit of protecting environmental resources).

President Clinton, despite questioning the benefits of NAFTA in the 1992 presidential campaign, adopted the idea of a Free Trade Area of the Americas (FTAA). To promote the new policies for the region, the Clinton administration developed the mechanism of presidential summits in the hemisphere. The agenda of the first Summit of the Americas in Miami (1994) called for a hemisphere-wide pact by the year 2005. U.S. policy for the region would thus officially focus on economic issues, though a concern with the drug wars threatened to overwhelm policy (see the next section).

Impact of Globalization on Chile

Although the world economy is not divided into three blocks, Europe and Asia-Pacific do offer markets that can mitigate dependence upon the U.S. market in the areas of trade and finance. Latin American countries have long sought this international diversification, but Chile has come a long way toward achieving it.

This diversification is not merely the result of market forces at work. Chile's democratic government adopted an explicit policy of ending the pariah status of the country. Chief among the means used to pursue this goal were bilateral free trade agreements and membership in multilateral economic groupings such as the Asia-Pacific Economic Council.

At the same time, the process of globalization has created new opportunities for Chile to insert itself into the international economy. This process began in the late 1970s, but Chilean policy errors made the economy extremely vulnerable to short-term capital flight, and the economy crashed in 1982. Subsequently, foreign economic policy adjusted, and Chile became a "darling" of international capital. The economy was strong enough to weather first the Mexican peso crisis of 1994 and then the Asian crisis of 1997.

Economic opening became a *política de estado* with the return of democracy. The democrats did not question whether to keep the economy open. Every major sector in Chile agreed on the necessity of deepening, broadening, and stabilizing the national economy's integration into the world economy. Consequently, the focus of Chilean trade policy continued to be the promotion of nondiscrimination, transparency, efficiency, and the development of comparative advantages. However, consensus on these general goals did not eliminate disagreements within Chile over the specific policies and terms of that integration. (See the discussion in Chapter Three.)

Chile has taken advantage of many of the new opportunities created by the globalization process. Under the military regime, Chile sought integration into world markets on its own, via unilateral policies of deregulating its economy. Though these measures were very successful, policy-makers in the new government believed that the benefits from unilaterally lowering tariffs were exhausted. In addition, the two Concertación governments sought a strategy to promote the comprehensive reintegration of Chile into international life. One of the mechanisms for this new policy was membership in new international and regional groupings. The multilateral character of these organizations meant that any rules regarding international economic interactions that were created or strengthened would cover more markets than would be possible with bilateral or subregional agreements. Membership in GATT and subsequently the World Trade Organization (WTO) has benefited the Chilean economy.

Although a less ideal path than the global route, joining economic groups or negotiating bilateral free trade pacts did provide a means of diversifying Chilean foreign economic relations and defending its export-import interests in those markets. Chief among these measures are a free trade agreement with Mexico in 1999, a series of bilateral agreements with Argentina,[27] and joining Mercosur as an associate member in 1997.[28]

Illustrative of Chilean prudence in its foreign economic policy was its decision not to become a full member of Mercosur, and thus subject to its common external tariff, until Mercosur countries lowered their tariffs to the levels of Chile's. There was also a concern that the Mercosur economies, especially Brazil's, were not yet sufficiently stable to warrant such close ties. By 2000 a closer association with Mercosur had become more likely, because reforms within the trade and integration pact had brought it closer to Chile's commercial policy. Newly elected

President Ricardo Lagos has also suggested that there should be closer ties between Mercosur and NAFTA.

Given these international economic goals, Chile responded quickly and positively to President Bush's proposal for hemispheric free trade in 1990. A multilateral project constituted an efficient means for opening and stabilizing regional markets for goods and investments (Chilean private investors were increasingly active in the hemisphere). In addition, there was a hope that a good working relationship on the Enterprise Initiative for the Americas would facilitate resolution of the remaining points of controversy on the Chile-U.S. agenda, especially those regarding nontariff barriers and seasonal increases in U.S. tariffs on Chilean agricultural exports. On October 1, 1990, Chile became the first Latin American country to sign a framework agreement with the U.S.

Giving priority to the U.S. Enterprise Initiative carried opportunity costs for Chile's foreign economic policy. Upon assuming office, the Aylwin government focused its attention on recovering Chile's place in Latin America, reducing its regional trade deficit and developing investment opportunities in neighboring countries. Bush's offer meant that Chile had to choose between working with some or all Latin American countries on a joint response or developing Chile's own unilateral response.

A joint response depended upon other Latin American countries reaching the degree of economic liberalization and structural adjustment already achieved by Chile. Consequently, this policy option promised fewer immediate economic benefits than would a successful bilateral negotiation with the United States. Of course, this bilateral route did not mean Chile would have to suspend negotiations with other Latin American countries, only that they would have a lower priority for government negotiators and could not become obstacles to negotiations with the United States.

There were initial successes in Chile's negotiations with the United States. In March of 1991 President Bush announced that Chile's accession to NAFTA (the FTAA was hemisphere-wide) would be handled under the "fast-track" authority granted by Congress to the executive. Under this rubric, Congress would refrain from considering modifications to the agreement and would vote simply on whether to accept or reject the treaty as negotiated by the executive. This legislation speeded up consideration of trade agreements and made them more likely to be approved. Chile was also able to reduce its governmental foreign debt. Ultimately, however, the U.S. Congress refused to renew the executive's fast-track authority, and Chilean membership in NAFTA was put on indefinite hold. (Chapter Six examines the NAFTA fiasco in detail.)

International Institutions and Regimes

Institutions themselves do not determine action; rather, they provide a context and a set of expectations or rules within which social interaction occurs. Both the historical-sociological and rational-choice approaches to institutions claim that institutions affect the incentives facing actors and structure the relations of power between groups, thereby affecting their behavior.[29] Institutional change may take many forms. A regime[30] may be created to deal with an issue area that had previously lacked a regime. In addition, a current regime may be strengthened, weakened, or even eliminated.

Economic Development

Institutions became a major factor in the international system after World War II. The United Nations was created to replace the failed League of Nations. Institutions were set up to deal with developing markets (the International Bank for Reconstruction and Development, also known as the World Bank), balance of payments crises (the International Monetary Fund, IMF), and trade (the General Agreement on Tariffs and Trade, GATT). These latter institutions, generally known as the Bretton Woods system, underwent major modifications beginning in the 1970s as the demands of globalization called for modifications in many of the rules underpinning the old system. The IMF in particular underwent an important change in altering its focus from stabilization to structural adjustment.

The Washington Consensus that guides U.S. policy toward Latin America has experienced some modification as a result of an incipient regime of "Summitry."[31] The first Summit of the Americas accepted the Washington Consensus as the basis of an economic development strategy that would dramatically diminish poverty as a result of foreign investment and labor-intensive exports.

Although poverty indices initially declined as a result of taming inflation, unemployment and employment in the informal sector grew in many countries of the region. Economic growth turned out to be dependent upon the export of natural resources, and the wage disparity between skilled and unskilled labor broadened. Economic insecurity for both the poor and the middle classes grew as a result of the insecurity of working conditions and the volatility of incomes.

A hemispheric meeting on development, held in Montevideo, Uruguay, in 1997, concluded that additional reforms were necessary. In a declaration titled "The Long March," participants called for investment in human resources, the promotion of efficient and solid financial markets, and improvement in the normative and legal environment (especially in labor markets and the regulation of private investment in infrastructure and social services). In addition, there was an emphasis on improving the quality of the public sector (including the judicial sector) as well as consolidating macroeconomic stability by strengthening the fiscal sector. These reforms require important and new institutional reforms.

The Second Summit of the Americas, on April 18, 1998, produced the "Santiago Consensus." Ambitious goals on educational, financial, judicial, and public-sector reforms were added to the economic focus of the Washington Consensus. Latin

Americans believe that the hemispheric consensus now centers on these more social aspects. How Washington will respond remains to be seen.

The end of the Cold War appears to have spurred further development and expansion of international institutions. We have already discussed some of those institutional factors in the section on globalization. Here we examine the other major policy arenas in which Chile is active and in which international institutions exist or are in the process of being created.

Security

There is an incipient regime in the hemisphere in the security arena. It is not yet clear whether the regime will find itself stillborn, become simply a tool of U.S. foreign policy (as was the infamous Inter-American Treaty of Reciprocal Assistance [Rio Treaty] of Cold War days), or succeed in becoming a truly cooperative security regime. At the regional level, the agreements and resolutions passed by the Organization of American States (OAS), the Group of Eight (formerly known as the Rio Group), and Mercosur demonstrate a clear and greater willingness of states to cede more jurisdiction to multilateral institutions than during the Cold War. In particular, the decision to elevate the defense of democracy to the level of a regional security threat demanding action by the inter-American community would have been inconceivable during the Cold War. The willingness of the community to act has been tested in Peru in 1992 to 1993 and 2000, Guatemala in 1993, Paraguay in 1999, and Ecuador in 2000. Only in the case of Haiti, in which the United States was eager to use military force to defend democracy, and of Peru in 2000 did Latin American governments shy away from international action in defense of democracy.[32]

Chile has been an important advocate for the creation of a confidence-building regime even as it modernizes and increases its own defense capabilities. Its unilateral policies in this arena have also been oriented in this direction, as evidenced by publication of the aforementioned Defense White Paper.[33] The Chile Defense Ministry and Armed Forces maintain a very active bilateral contact and exchange of information with their counterparts in neighboring countries. With respect to conflict resolution, Chilean policy supports hemispheric efforts and Chile was a participant in the 1995 to 1998 negotiations that ended the Ecuador-Peru border dispute.[34] But Chile cannot support imposing a resolution to a dispute, given the ongoing controversy with Bolivia over sovereign access to the Pacific Ocean.

Human Rights, Including Democracy

The democratic governments of Chile have been enthusiastic defenders of human rights conventions and the defense of democracy. The Concertación governments have perceived that these international and regional regimes provide international support for Chilean democracy against its domestic critics. These international norms and conventions may increase the political weight of domestic reformers who seek to extend Chile's democracy beyond the limits negotiated during the transition from military rule.

Some analysts may see a certain irony, therefore, in the Frei administration asserting the primacy of national sovereignty and dignity in response to international efforts to bring General Pinochet to trial in Europe from 1998 to 2000. The position of the Chilean government was not, however, a rejection of international human rights principles. The Frei administration opposed the notion of extraterritoriality in general, whether that is U.S. legislation against Cuba in the Helms-Burton law or international law on human rights. Any violations of international law, the Frei administration argued, should be prosecuted in the countries in which those violations are purported to have occurred.

The Pinochet case attracted great attention in the United States, and its final resolution will undoubtedly affect Chilean-U.S. relations. Table 2.4 illustrates coverage of the case in nine major U.S. newspapers and magazines from the time of the general's arrest in October 1998 until his return to Chile in March 2000. The table demonstrates the wide range of issues noted in the headlines of the articles on the case, including the arrest itself, international law, the role of the U.S. government, the official position of the Chilean government, and the impact of the case on Chile itself.

The potential consequences of the Pinochet case have been discussed extensively. Some Republican congressmen have pronounced themselves against the increased scope of international criminal courts. These policy-makers fear that the expansion of international law and this type of tribunal could tie the hands of U.S. leaders by raising the possibility of their being judged for official acts once they leave office.[35]

While Pinochet was detained in London, the U.S. government did not pronounce itself clearly one way or another on the issue. Upon his return to Chile in March 2000, the Clinton administration requested that investigations in the Letelier case resume: "According to the federal laws of the United States and the laws of the District of Colombia there is no statue of limitations for murder or some of the other crimes still unsolved. Consequently, the warrants against those individuals with accusations outstanding, and any other person who might have been implicated in the murders that occurred in the United States, have not expired with the passage of time."[36] The United States received permission to interrogate forty-two people.

Thirty-six U.S. congressmen asked President Clinton to request at a Berlin summit that President Lagos facilitate the extradition of General Pinochet himself in the case. In their letter the congressmen indicated: "we believe that the man who gave the order to assassinate—General Augusto Pinochet—remains at large."[37]

Between March and June 2000, numerous articles appeared in the principal newspapers concerning the involvement of the military government in human

TABLE 2.4

General Pinochet's Detention in London
U.S. News Headlines 1998–2000

Themes / Months	Total	Cases Reported	International Law	Role of U.S.	Chile: Domestic Impact	Chile: Official Position
October '98	56	28	13	6	4	5
November	63	27	9	9	11	7
December	37	24	3	6	4	-
January '99	39	26	4	5	2	2
February	17	7	6	1	3	-
March	47	34	5	1	7	-
April	15	9	-	-	6	-
May	10	7	-	-	3	-
August	14	7	-	2	2	3
September	8	2	-	1	4	1
October	37	25	2	1	9	-
November	13	10	3	-	-	-
December	15	14	-	1	-	-
January 2000	59	23	4	1	30	-
March	36	5	2	1	28	-
Total	**466**	**248**	**51**	**35**	**114**	**18**

Sources: FLACSO-Chile calculations from articles in the *Chicago Tribune*, the *New York Times*, the *Los Angeles Times*, the *Orlando Sentinel*, the *Boston Globe*, the *Washington Post*, *USA Today*, the *Washington Times*, *Newsday* (New Jersey).

rights violations. New information was revealed about the 1973 cases of Charles Horman (which inspired the movie *Missing*) and Frank Teruggi and the 1985 case of Boris Weisfeiler. In June, the U.S. government requested that the Chilean government provide information about these cases. U.S. human rights NGOs have also claimed that U.S. government organizations have more information about these cases, and they are requesting that the material be declassified.[38] (The "Postscript" contains more information on Pinochet and human rights.)

The Drug Trade

Stimulated by U.S. pressure, but also increasingly desired by some Latin American governments under siege by the drug cartels and networks, an antidrug regime has been developing in fits and starts.[39] Chile is not a producing country, but it has increasingly become a locus for transshipment and money laundering, especially as the northern routes out of the Andes and to the United States become increasingly risky for the trade. The country's export boom also facilitates drug trafficking. The Chilean government has initiated strong domestic programs

TABLE 2.5

Consumption of Illicit Drugs in Chile (Percentage of population)

Type	1994	1996	1998
Marijuana	4.00	4.01	4.73
Pasta base	0.86	0.63	0.81
Cocaine	0.90	0.83	1.32

Source: Comisión Nacional de Control de Estupefacientes (CONACE), Estudio nacional de consumo de drogas, 1994, 1996, and 1998.

to combat illicit trade. Unlike most other Latin American countries, the strength and abilities of the Chilean police force make the support of the armed forces unnecessary in fighting Chile's drug problems. The fact that the Chilean drug trafficking problem is relatively inconsequential as of this writing makes Chilean regional initiatives and cooperation unnecessary.[40]

Chile sees the problem of drugs chiefly as a health issue. Nevertheless, the increased flow of drugs through Chile is beginning to create domestic problems. The usual crime and violence associated with narcotrafficking is on the rise. The nation is particularly concerned with the upward trend in drug consumption among young people (see Table 2.5).

Conclusion

The international context within which the Chilean-U.S. relationship occurs changed dramatically with the end of the Cold War. Yet the Cold War only indirectly affected the dynamics of this particular bilateral relationship; international factors set a context for the interaction among states. Some broad policy decisions in the Chilean-U.S. relationship can be explained simply by examining the international context and the positions of the two actors in it.

The international context has changed in ways compatible with a new political system in Chile and continuation of the military government's economic development strategy. Chile thus confronts many new opportunities, some of which facilitate more cooperative relations with the United States. Thus the two countries work together on most issues, especially in the areas of security and trade. Yet, reflective of their different international position, what they bring to and want from the relationship are not identical. A bilateral relationship reflects how much each side needs the other and what priority a partner is willing to give the bilateral relationship in its general international politics. The United States "needs" Chile far less than Chile "needs" the unipolar power. Chile has responded prudently by seeking both better relations with the United States and continued diversification of its international politics.

Points of friction and foregone opportunities nevertheless continue to exist in the Chile-U.S. relationship. To understand why some *políticas de estado* fail or undergo significant modification, we need to move beyond recognizing the existence of international opportunities. Whether governments can make effective use of those opportunities is largely explained at the domestic level where interest groups, bureaucracies, and nongovernmental actors influence policy. It is to those factors that we turn in subsequent chapters.

THREE

DOMESTIC FACTORS IN FOREIGN POLICY

FOREIGN POLICY IS HEAVILY INFLUENCED BY DOMESTIC politics. Even advocates of a systemic view of international politics recognize that to explain how states react to international constraints and opportunities requires a theory of foreign policy in which domestic factors play key roles.[1] The challenge for analysts of foreign policy lies in identifying the relevant domestic factors and how they influence policy in conjunction with international factors.

In this chapter we lay out the domestic institutional and societal factors that help in understanding Chile's policies toward the United States and vice versa. We focus on the processes by which foreign policy is developed. These processes are guided by formal constitutional and legislative rules, as well as by bureaucratic processes and interest group politics. These foreign policy processes affect the choice of policy and therefore its continuity over time and across issues.

In Chile, the outward-oriented and pro–private sector economic focus is institutionalized in the constitutional structures. Since Chile is now a democracy, any changes to these orientations would have to be undertaken through the requisite constitutional reforms. Current institutional and coalition politics make any major changes highly unlikely, thereby both pushing the government to seek to deepen international economic relations and making the country more credible in the agreements it undertakes internationally. Institutional factors in the United States make its foreign policy process very transparent to its foreign interlocutors. The struggles between the executive and legislative branches in particular shed light on the bargaining range for U.S. foreign policy and make any policies adopted by the country more credible to U.S. partners and rivals.

We argue in this chapter that domestic institutional and political factors affect collaboration between the two countries. Cooperation on security issues, the consolidation of democracy, and the promotion of greater economic openness internationally have been enhanced by these domestic factors. At the same time, the relationship has been complicated on bilateral trade and, to a lesser extent, human rights.

The substantive portions of the chapter are organized into two sections. In the first section we examine the domestic institutional context that structures foreign policy making. Although both countries are modern democracies, they differ on important ways in which institutional rules affect the ability of citizens to influence politicians. A second section examines the political coalitions behind each government to ascertain the specific interests that presidents in each country will try to address, and by which they will be constrained.

The Domestic Institutional Structure of Foreign Policy

Chile and the United States are both democracies. We can expect, therefore, that the citizenry will influence foreign policy. Yet we must remember that modern democracies limit popular sovereignty by laws and institutions. It is inherent in the nature of laws and institutions that groups with certain resources will have advantages over groups lacking such resources. To the degree that foreign policy is affected by domestic politics, these inherent biases will affect the bilateral relationship.

In this section we focus on how these democracies are constituted, not which is the "purer" democracy. Chile and the United States have distinct institutional structures of democracy. Consequently, who participates, how, and with what degree of influence vary across the two countries. We therefore want to keep an eye out for the biases inherent in each institutional structure and take cognizance of their potential impact on foreign policy.

Chile

The institutional structure of contemporary Chilean politics is set by the Constitution of 1980, approved by a plebiscite during the military government but accepted by the democratic parties as a price of the transition to democracy. In addition, the continuity of the traditional political party system after 1990 affects the articulation of popular demands. These two institutional characteristics of the Chilean political system limit democracy in important ways but also contribute to stable democratic politics and policy continuities.

The 1980 Constitution was designed to "protect" capitalist democracy once the military left power. It does so via four major institutions, currently labeled by critics as the "authoritarian enclaves." These are a Supreme Court linked over time to the court in office at the time of transition, an electoral system designed to favor the status quo, the creation of "designated" (i.e., nonelected) senators, and a high degree of autonomy for the armed forces.

Article 75 of Chapter VI of the 1980 Constitution stipulates that the Justices of the Supreme Court will be nominated by the president and confirmed by two thirds of the Senate. The president, however, may nominate someone only from a list of five persons selected by the sitting Court itself. The Senate must confirm the nomination by a two-thirds majority.

Chilean law provides those over eighteen years of age with the obligation to register and vote. Chileans vote on Sunday. There have been four major elections since the 1988 plebiscite. The results are presented in Table 3.1.

Electoral changes increased the political influence of the right. Rural areas (more favorable to the right) are overrepresented in the Chamber of Deputies,

TABLE 3.1

Major Chilean National Elections 1988–2000

Plebiscite 1988	Presidential 1989	Presidential 1993	Presidential 2000 (2nd round)
No 54.71%	Patricio Aylwin 55.17%	Eduardo Frei 58.01% Other center-left (Pizarro, Reitze, MacHeff) 11.41%	Ricardo Lagos 51.32%
Yes 43.01%	Hermán Büchi 29.40% Fco. Errázuriz 15.43%	Arturo Alessandri 24.39% José Piñera 6.18%	Joaquín Lavín 48.68%

to the detriment of urban voters (where the center-left does better). In fact, the lines of districts (deputies) and regions (senators) were gerrymandered to over-represent voters who favored Pinochet in the 1988 plebiscite.[2]

The rules governing representation promote the creation of political alliances during the electoral campaign, thereby forcing the socialist left toward the center if it desires to participate in governing. Unlike the prior Constitution of 1925, a presidential candidate must now win a majority of the electoral votes. If none of the candidates receives such a total, a second round among the top two vote recipients is held. In legislative elections, each district or region elects two deputies or senators. One seat goes to the leading vote-getter, but for the second seat to go to the same party it must get two thirds of the total vote or double the total of its nearest competitor.[3] A minority party can thus theoretically gain 50 percent of the seats in the legislature.

These particular electoral rules at present favor the right because the center-left coalition dominates the elections. But should a center-right coalition emerge (as in the 1964 elections), the left should find itself favored by the same rules. Thus, rather than overemphasize their specific impact on the right's political influence at present, it is better to note that these electoral rules make it difficult for any winning coalition to make policy without gaining some consent from the opposition.

The Constitution provides for nine "designated" senators in addition to the thirty-eight selected in general elections. Article 45 specifies that four are to be chosen by the National Security Council (NSC) from among the retired commanders in chief of the three military branches plus the national police. The Supreme Court chooses three, two from its retired justices and one from retired attorneys general. The president selects another two, one from former cabinet ministers and another from the former rectors of an officially recognized university. The forty-seven-member Senate is then filled out by the addition of all presidents of the republic who have served six year terms (Aylwin's tenure was limited to four years); these former presidents become "senators for life." In 1999 General

Pinochet retired as commander in chief of the army and assumed his seat as senator for life, based upon his tenure as president from 1980 to 1990.

Given the large majorities required for constitutional amendments, this initial stacking of the Senate in favor of the right effectively limits the scope of constitutional change. Designated senators also serve as a force for consensus policy-making because both houses of Congress (as in the United States) must approve legislation. Yet the long-term impact of the designated senators is less clear. Since the Concertación won the 1999 election with a left candidate, the center-left will govern for at least the first sixteen years of the new democracy. The composition of designated senators should change as a result. Given the manner in which the Supreme Court is selected, it will likely be a long time before the type of members nominated by the Court change. But we should see changes elsewhere. The two cabinet and university rector designees will have been selected by the Concertación. There will be retired commanders in chief of the armed forces and national police who will not have been intimates of Pinochet. In addition, Pinochet will probably have died while Frei and Lagos will be senators for life. If a center-left coalition wins in 2006 it should have the votes in the Senate to accomplish important constitutional change. Alternatively, the left may have the ability to block much of the legislation attempted by a government of the center-right after 2006.

The Constitution assigns three roles to the armed forces: the Chilean military is the defender of national sovereignty; protector of national security; and guarantor of the institutional order (Article 90). This last element, absent before 1980, allows the armed forces to participate actively in the National Security Council, and through it, in domestic and foreign policy.

The National Security Council was created by the 1980 Constitution. The voting members of the Security Council are the president of the Republic, president of the Senate, president of the Supreme Court, commanders in chief of the air force, navy, and army, the general director of the National Police (Carabineros), and the attorney general. Members who can speak but not vote include ministers of the interior, external relations, defense, economics, and finance. The Security Council's secretary is the joint chief of staff of defense.[4]

The purpose of the Security Council is to advise the president, upon request, on matters of national security. The council also has the responsibility to express its views to the president, the National Congress, and the Constitutional Tribune concerning an event that, in the council's view, constitutes a grave threat to the institutions of government or could compromise national security. The council also reports on the status of the armed forces, collects information related to external and internal security from relevant authorities and functionaries, and performs any other functions that the Constitution stipulates. The latter attribute refers to the nomination of the designated senators.[5]

The Security Council has met sporadically, sometimes regarding formal and routine topics and at other times addressing more political themes. In effect, it represents a means by which the military can pressure civilian government. It has met only four times on matters of foreign policy. The first was a routine matter of permitting foreign troops into Chilean territory, and the latter three pertained to the Pinochet detention. The Security Council has never met on a matter dealing with the United States.

The Security Council can be convoked by the president or by two of its members. Meetings require a quorum of a majority of its members. The council, therefore, is not under the complete control of the president. Each of the three Concertación governments (Aylwin, Frei, and now Lagos) has attempted constitutional reforms that would significantly modify the Security Council. The major changes would turn the council into simply an advisory agency for the president and would eliminate its ability to pass resolutions.

The Constitution also guarantees the military a minimum budget: it cannot fall below the level of the military government's last year in office (1989, in real terms) plus the rate of inflation. Added to the stipulation about the tenure of commanders in chief, this budget proviso creates a significant limitation on the degree to which a civilian government might "discipline" the military. The democratic governments, however, have turned this into a ceiling as well: although the economy boomed from 1990 to 1998, the military budget did not expand.[6]

The Constitution deprives the president of the traditional power to control the appointment of the highest military authorities. The commanders in chief at the end of the military regime (including Pinochet as army commander in chief) were allowed to hold their positions for four more years. The president may not remove commanders in chief from their posts during their four-year terms without the express consent of the National Security Council. The commanders of the respective branches of the armed forces each nominate the five senior officers for promotion. The president of the Republic selects the new commander from the list, and the commander may not serve a second term.

The involvement of the armed forces in the political system is institutionalized but, to be effective, requires the political support of civilian groups that share its goals. Because the legitimacy of modifying the 1980 Constitution is no longer in question, the military has been obliged to build alliances to protect certain of its features that, in its view, are essential to maintaining the institutional order.

When speaking of military autonomy, one must distinguish among the different branches of the armed forces. The behavior of the army, air force, and navy differs in important ways. The army has played an active role, highlighted by the presence of General Pinochet, while the air force and navy have played only minor roles. By focusing its activities on professional concerns, the navy in particular has maintained good relations with the democratic administrations and appears to have played an auxiliary role in the two peaceful changes of command since 1989.

The Constitution guarantees private property (Article 19) and severely limits the ability of the state to expropriate it. It also limits the ability of the state to act as an entrepreneur, in particular by making the Central Bank independent of the president. No public expense or loan may be financed by credits from the Central Bank. The autonomous Central Bank can engage in financial transactions only with public or private financial institutions.[7] Only in cases of war or similar danger can the Central Bank provide or give financial credits to the state or to public and private nonfinancial entities. As a result, one of the major cleavages in precoup Chile (whether the state can displace the private sector) has been eliminated in contemporary Chile.

The president is in charge of foreign relations, and the 1980 Constitution did not alter the traditionally limited role of Congress in this policy arena. The president designates diplomatic posts and representatives to international organizations without the need for congressional ratification.[8] The president may travel internationally without congressional authorization, except if he will be absent for more than thirty days or in the last ninety days of the administration.[9] The president also directs political relations with other foreign powers and organizations. The executive branch negotiates treaties, which are subject to approval without modification by Congress. Congressional deliberations on these issues may be secret if the president desires. The president may also enter into international agreements and adopt domestic administrative policies without congressional authorization if the agreements and policies are for the purposes of implementing treaties ratified by Congress and do not imply making new laws. Congress has the power to declare war, but the president is the one who proposes the declaration.[10] The president must also consult with the National Security Council before making such a proposal.

Congress has become increasingly dissatisfied that in this era of globalization it can only approve without modification or reject a treaty negotiated by the executive branch. Congress feels that since many of these treaties are now becoming binding on domestic law, it should have a role in negotiating Chilean accession to these treaties. The issue has become particularly contentious in the case of human rights treaties because some provisions contradict Chile's amnesty law.

In summary, the Chilean political institutional structure is a powerful force promoting consensus policy-making. The scope of change is thereby limited, and the political polarization that characterized Chilean politics before 1973 is mitigated. This institutional structure also makes the implementation of whatever policy is adopted more likely. Consequently, the credibility of Chile as an international partner has been enhanced by the combination of the institutional structure guiding Chilean politics and its redemocratization.

The United States

The foreign policy process in the United States reflects the underlying theme of the U.S. philosophy of power: dividing power and making leaders accountable to the electorate is the only way to ensure democratic control of power. Thus the

Constitution gives the legislative and executive branches independent yet overlapping voices, and even the Supreme Court can weigh in on policy disputes at times. Some issues are reserved for state jurisdiction, while others are federal. And politicians in the federal government are subject to constituencies at three levels: local (House), state (Senate) and national (president).

The U.S. electoral system affects which citizen voices are heard in the political arena. The single-member district and winner-takes-all nature of U.S. elections promote the movement of candidates to the center and the development of a two-party system. Minority views on either side of the political spectrum have significantly less representation in the U.S. Congress than if the United States had a parliamentary system or a presidential system like Chile's. The cost of electoral campaigning in the contemporary era (the two major candidates for one of California's Senate seats spent $44.4 million in 1994[11]) certainly raises a large barrier for potential candidates and smaller parties.

There are other electoral mechanisms that historically and in the contemporary period affect how constrained politicians are by the citizenry. Senators were once elected indirectly by state legislators. The president is actually elected by the Electoral College rather than by a direct popular vote. States receive delegates to the college in proportion to the population, and delegates are usually normatively but not legally bound to vote for the candidate that won in their state. Four times in U.S. history, including in 2000, the candidate that won the popular vote did not become president because he lost in the Electoral College. If no candidate attains the requisite 270 votes to win in the college, the House chooses among the top three candidates, with each state delegation receiving only one vote.[12]

Since elections are held on a working day, Tuesday, rather than Sunday, voter turnout by the working class in particular is negatively affected. In the 2000 election, the polls closed in St. Louis with long lines of people deprived of their chance to vote.[13] There are undoubtedly other reasons in addition to the winner-takes-all nature of elections and the specific voting day to explain low voter registration and turnout in the United States. The point is, however, that the president may represent the majority of those who voted in a particular election but not necessarily a majority of those eligible to vote or even of those registered to vote. In 1980, 53 percent of registered voters went to the polls. Ronald Reagan received 50.7 percent of those votes. Consequently, he became president with the votes of less than 27 percent of registered voters.[14]

Gerrymandering also occurs in the United States. State legislators redraw electoral boundaries after the census every decade. The party that controls the legislature often utilizes bizarre boundaries to create districts with characteristics more favorable to producing electoral victories by that party. The Supreme Court has ruled against particularly egregious instances of gerrymandering, but the general practice continues to influence how votes matter.[15]

Although the legislators are subject to periodic election, this does not translate into direct popular control over every action taken by a congressperson. Rather, it is the overall record of voting, and in particular on those issues of most concern to their constituency, that politicians attempt to keep in line with their constituencies' desires. Hence politicians may vote against some policies favored by their constituencies. The Senate voted against the Comprehensive Nuclear Test Ban Treaty in 1999 although polls indicated that a majority of the public supported it.[16] And although campaign finance reform is popular among the public and is subject to some regulation, neither the House nor the Senate seems interested in plugging the loopholes that allow corporations and labor unions, among others, indirectly to channel funds to candidates.[17]

The executive carries out foreign policy, including negotiating treaty commitments. Yet Congress has powerful means to influence foreign policy. Since the Senate must approve treaties by a supermajority of two thirds, negotiations are effectively constrained by the positions that senators communicate to the executive branch before and during the negotiations. Congress also controls the budget and can refuse to fund any foreign policy it chooses. Consequently, when the president and his aides are engaged in international negotiations, they are playing a "two-level game": negotiations with another country overlap with negotiations being carried out with the relevant political forces at home.[18]

Congress can delegate some of its decision-making power to the executive, but such delegation is always subject to recall if the executive's relative freedom of action displeases Congress. Congressional "oversight" is carried out through a variety of mechanisms, ranging from constituency appeals, through a legislator's personal fact-finding with office staffs or via personal activity, to holding hearings and calling executive branch officers to testify.

A relevant example for the U.S.-Chilean relationship of delegation and oversight is "fast-track" legislation for trade agreements. Congress has periodically provided the executive a relatively free rein to negotiate trade agreements by binding itself to approve or reject the agreement as presented. But "fast-track" legislation was subject to renewal, and in 1998 Congress refused to extend it. Faced with a probable plethora of amendments by Congress contrary to what U.S. and Chilean negotiators would likely agree upon, President Clinton opted to postpone negotiating a treaty to incorporate Chile into NAFTA.

Within Congress, minority voices can effectively block or severely modify legislation because of the committee structure and each chamber's rules governing filibusters and the amendment process. In 1995 Senator Jesse Helms (R-N.C.) became chairman of the Senate Foreign Relations Committee. His personal values (clearly representing a minority view in the United States) and personal animosity toward President Clinton led him effectively to hold up the appointment of many ambassadorships.

The executive has its own prerogatives in foreign policy. Although the Senate must approve treaties, the president can enter into executive agreements without the consent of Congress. These agreements even include the commitment of the United States government to come to the military defense of the partner to the agreement. They may also be classified and therefore kept secret from Congress. During the Cold War the number of executive agreements outnumbered treaties by more than twenty to one.[19]

The executive's ability to make foreign policy was enhanced at the beginning of the Cold War and has not been reduced since its termination. Prior to this time, the president relied on a poorly staffed Department of State and personal advisors for advice in foreign affairs. The 1947 National Security Act created a huge bureaucracy to aid the president in defense-related policy. The War Department did not downsize, as was the norm after a U.S. war, but became the Department of Defense, housed in the largest building in the world, the Pentagon. The Central Intelligence Agency (CIA) was created, with a secret budget that is known in general terms only by the Senate and House Intelligence Committees; the Pentagon also has its Defense Intelligence Agency (DIA). The National Security Council was created to "advis(e) the President with respect to the integration of domestic, foreign and military policies relating to the national security."[20]

Such a bureaucracy has not proven to be an unmitigated good for the president. Bureaucratic politics and infighting in the executive branch are well known and publicized, extending even to CIA-DIA rivalry.[21] The bureaucracies use their expertise and control over information to compete for resources, influence, and autonomy. Bureaucratic competition is further stimulated by civilian politicians who see even intelligence and military issue areas as fair game for scoring political points against their competitors.

The military is a special type of bureaucratic actor in the United States. It is clearly subordinate to civilian control in general terms, and some concerns have been expressed about the ability of the military to influence policy. In the 1950s there was fear, even expressed by President (and retired five-star general) Dwight D. Eisenhower, of a military-industrial complex powerful enough to sway national policy toward its particular interests.[22] The influence of the military-industrial complex has been partly diminished because civilian politicians and their staffs have expertise on these matters and can also tap into private think tanks specializing in security issues.

The withdrawal from the debacle in Vietnam eased many concerns about the power of the military. Under President Reagan's renewed emphasis on military power and with an active secretary of defense, however, the military seemed to recover some degree of policy influence. In 1984 Casper W. Weinberger laid out the conditions under which the military should be used in support of foreign policy. Weinberger, a civilian, articulated a perspective representing a military organization's point of view. Congress subsequently gave the military a direct voice in foreign policy by making the chairman of the joint chiefs of staff an official member of the National Security Council in 1986. Military spokespeople now refer in the press to these conditions defined by Weinberger, trying to influence when and how the president will choose to use them. For many analysts in the United States, this has become a means by which the military is whittling away at its subordination to civilian control embodied in the president.[23]

Political Coalitions and Foreign Policy

Chile

Until the return of democracy in 1990, technocrats and the dictator Pinochet dominated the national planning process. After the economic collapse of 1982, national capital gained more influence, but broad domestic political coalitions continued to be effectively excluded from influencing policy. With the return of democracy, national planning, including foreign policy, has become the result of an interaction among the legislative and executive branches and interest groups in society. A specific policy is chosen when coalitions favoring a policy outweigh, in political terms, those opposed to it.

These coalitions express opinions rooted in a complex network of ideological, strategic, economic, and political views. In contemporary Chile, two major political coalitions express the aspirations of a majority of Chilean society. These competing perspectives—one "corporatist" and the other "democratic-modernizing"—for Chile's foreign policy reflect political alliances that cut across every dimension of Chilean society, including the civil-military division.

The first coalition has a corporatist vision. Its championing of "protected democracy," which materialized in the 1980 Constitution, marks its ideology. In rough electoral terms, the coalition can be characterized as the 43 percent of the vote in the 1988 plebiscite that sought to retain General Augusto Pinochet as president. This opposition group shrank to 30 percent in the 1993 presidential election and rose to 48.7 percent in the second round of the 2000 elections. (This latter figure was inflated by the PDC members of the center-left coalition who could not bring themselves to vote for a former socialist.) In the new democratic era, the best safeguard for the interests of this coalition is defense of the current constitutional structure.

The corporatist coalition is distrustful of economic integration, both at the regional level (Mercosur) and with the United States. The corporatist position presupposes that Chile's accession to a regional bloc would affect aspects of its national defense. Thus the opening of the Chilean economy to international markets is accepted but brings with it a distrust of accords that imply complete interdependence. Many of the political conflicts over the content of foreign policy focus on how the corporatist ideology can fit into and coexist with the democratic system.

The views of a large segment of the political opposition, composed primarily of the Independent Democratic Union (Unión Demócrata Independiente, UDI) and a portion of the National Renewal Party (Renovación Nacional, RN), are represented by the corporatist coalition.[24] The UDI represents large businesses, business associations, and ultraconservative Catholics and is tightly linked with the former military regime. UDI has also achieved an important insertion in popular sectors. The RN represents a slightly more moderate political force but with similar links to the military regime. The more liberal segment of the RN is interested in deepening the democratic institutional framework.

The democratic-modernizers exemplify the main thrust of Chilean public opinion at the end of the twentieth century. The Concertación por la Democracia represents them. This coalition of political parties won 55 percent of the vote in the 1988 plebiscite and has won all three presidential elections, with Aylwin (1989), Frei Ruiz-Tagle (1993), and Lagos (1999).

The democratic-modernizers accept the institutional limitations set by the military government, but they follow its provisions to pursue the establishment of policies aimed at modifying those limitations. By working within the rules of the game as established during the democratic transition, the coalition has constructed a broad and substantive political consensus.

The most important goals of the democratic-modernizers are the mitigation of the social inequalities produced by the neoliberal development model, and the further democratization of the institutions inherited from the military regime. The leadership of this coalition recognizes that any changes in politics and economics must occur within the context of the current constitutional rules, including those for modifying the Constitution itself. The economic strategy therefore promotes economic growth and greater efficiency.[25] Achieving these goals permits distribution to the bottom end of the social structure without redistributing or attacking the resources claimed by the upper classes. The success of this policy has been dramatic: poverty levels fell from 38.6 percent in 1990 to 21.7 percent in 1998, while the level of extreme poverty fell over the same time period from 12.9 percent to 5.6 percent.[26]

The Concertación's foreign policy is designed to promote this domestic strategy of growth and distribution. As noted in Chapter Two, integration into international markets provides new opportunities for growth. That policy also makes the Latin American region a priority for Chile because of its proximity and untapped potential. But regional integration requires overcoming the colonial legacy of border conflicts. As a consequence, the search for regional peace and international security becomes important in Chile's foreign policy.[27]

Regional integration will facilitate Chile's development as a "port country," serving to transport goods from the markets on the eastern side of the Andes (Argentina, Bolivia, Paraguay, Uruguay, and Brazil) to Asia. Achieving this status will stimulate economic growth and bring the benefits of that growth to the southern and northern regions of the nation, where social justice has long been ignored.[28]

The foreign policy of the democratic-modernizers supports another domestic objective as well: the transformation of civil-military relations. The goal is the creation of an effective defense community, led by civilians and emphasizing the professionalization of the armed forces. In 1994, the administration of Eduardo Frei (1994–2000) announced its decision to create a clear-cut defense policy designed through a public, informed process, which it hoped would strengthen long-term commitments to the state's military policies. Officials in the Ministry of Defense set four goals: citizen commitment, state responsibility, a context of peace, and efficiency within the armed forces.[29] By decreasing the external threat, the Concertación hopes to diminish the military's political power at home as well as freeing up resources for development. Full attainment of this policy goal, however, will require constitutional reforms.[30]

The armed forces have their own views on defense policy. At the beginning of the political transition, the armed forces produced documents examining the position of Chile's combat institutions within the new international environment.[31] The individual reports of the navy (1990), air force (1991), and army (1992) emphasized different objectives, but all sought to consolidate their role within the new institutional framework by contributing to national defense and development. The navy made "sea presence" and maritime security its priorities. The air force developed an extensive space program based on the creation of an agency responsible for the launching of satellites and satellite communications. And since 1992 the army has advanced a plan "to conquer and consolidate control in Chile's interior frontiers" as a response to the need to improve the state's presence in marginalized and poverty-stricken zones within Chile.[32] The creation of these concepts indicates that the military, beyond attempting to justify its existence in the face of threatened budget cuts and lack of interest on the part of civil society, has tried to influence the development of public policy concerning specific strategic concepts.

The development of defense policy is limited by inadequate preparation on the part of civilians in the defense field. For many years, Chilean civilians did not participate in decision-making in defense matters. Between 1932 and 1973—a period of great democratic stability when there were few civil-military tensions—the notion took root that military matters should be handled exclusively by military personnel. After the military's discredited intervention in national politics in June 1932, the political elite viewed combat institutions as a specialized province where civilians can do little. This lack of interest in military matters on the part of the political class caused a general devaluation of the armed forces in the eyes of civilians. Many people came to believe that the mission of the armed forces is not relevant when compared to more pressing national problems, such as improving education, health, and living standards for the country's population. This neglect on the part of civil society provided the military with freedom to discuss and debate its own policies and even reformulate its mission.

The interactions among the two political coalitions dominating Chilean politics today are guided by two principles: the acceptance of a negotiated transition, and the "pact on governability." The negotiated transition to democracy involved relinquishing the polarization of the authoritarian period. Between 1985 and 1990, government and opposition slowly ceded ground to each other, allowing their relationship to evolve peacefully.[33] This process meant, however, that the military government would not be overthrown completely, nor would the democratic opposition win a clear victory. The military gave up power, but the new government authorities were forced to accept the constitutional limitations set during the Pinochet regime. This established a logic whereby any change to the political system requires negotiation among all the political actors represented in Congress.[34]

The success of the negotiated transition also depended on cooperation among the parties opposed to the military regime. The Social Democrats, the Radical Party, the Party of Democracy, and the Socialist Party (as well as a dozen other small groupings that revolved around these four main political organizations) created the Concertación alliance that coordinated the activities of all the opposition groups. The political leadership of these opposition parties realized that the nature of the electoral system and the number of competing parties precluded winning an absolute majority if they did not ally.

The pact on governability among opposing parties developed out of the process of reforming the political system and the institutional order. The pact is basically an agreement to disagree: competing views coexist, but there is consensus to avoid a level of political or social tension that would render the country ungovernable. As a result, the armed forces and the right, which believe the military government was a huge success, work with the center-left government, which is critical of the regime (especially of its human rights violations). The tension is strong, but both groups interact without destabilizing the institutions of government.[35]

The human rights issue demonstrates the strength of the pact on governability. The Aylwin administration's policy on human rights focused on uncovering the truth and carrying out justice "as far as was possible."[36] A Commission on Truth and Reconciliation was formed to find out the facts about the human rights violations and to channel cases through the judicial system. For the armed forces, this meant that human rights violators could be prosecuted, despite the existence of the Amnesty Law promulgated by the military government. In their view, it put the military regime itself on trial. In response, the armed forces published their version of the events between 1973 and 1990. Notably, this was not a collective interpretation. Each service delivered its own report, and they show the diversity of judgment used to assess the record on human rights. The army and navy reports focused on interpreting the historical record, whereas the air force looked more toward the future.[37]

When General Pinochet was arrested in London in 1998 on Spain's appeal for extradition on human rights violations, the pact faced another major challenge. The Frei government, led by Foreign Minister Jose Miguel Insulza, who had been exiled under the military regime, argued that Pinochet could not be tried in a foreign country for alleged crimes committed in Chile. The return of Pinochet to Chile allowed the justice tribunals to proceed in hearing the cases against him.

Over one hundred accusations were filed against the former chief of state in Chile. As a senator, Pinochet enjoyed immunity from prosecution. Since he holds the position of "Lifetime Senator" he could not be judged unless his immunity was removed. The Santiago Court of Appeals, by a vote of 13 to 9, stripped Pinochet of his immunity and the Supreme Court affirmed the decision. He was formally indicted and placed under house arrest in February 2001.

Parallel to the Pinochet case, Chilean society and the military itself have sought to develop new ways to resolve the issue of the disappeared and detained by the military government. After repeated failures by the Aylwin and Frei administrations to make progress on the issue, the Dialogue on Human Rights (Mesa de Diálogo sobre Derechos Humanos) achieved a breakthrough. President Lagos put significant political resources into reaching this accord to resolve a fundamental issue challenging national unity. In mid-June 2000, Congress passed a law establishing "professional secrecy privileges" for members of the four armed services, religious institutions, and the Masons, which will receive information on the disappeared for six months. Following a meeting of 156 retired Army generals, Fernando Paredes, president of the Retired Generals Association, made a significant announcement: "The time has come to free the new generation (of military officers) of the burdens of the past, for which they have no responsibility, and allow the country to attain the material and spiritual welfare it deserves."[38]

The United States

Because the institutional characteristics of U.S. politics push voters, and therefore politicians, toward the center of the political spectrum, the Clinton coalition was not radically distinct from that of any other person who might actually win a presidential election. This is especially true in periods of economic growth, international peace, and low crime. In addition, the division of power between the legislative and executive branches means that if two different parties control each branch of government, policy will have to reflect areas of agreement between the two political coalitions behind the parties.

Within the center of the U.S. political arena there are still important differences that affect policy, depending upon who is in office. Between the 1930s and 1980 the political coalition dominating U.S. politics was characterized as the New Deal coalition. Voters in this coalition wanted the federal government to take responsibility for the social and economic well-being of the population. Labor, farmers, urban poor, and African Americans in the northern part of the country proved to be the backbone of this coalition, and the Democratic Party benefited from their votes.

The New Deal coalition began to unravel in the 1980s, as the size of government and government subsidies for the poor became issues forcing Democratic politicians to package themselves as fiscally conservative but socially progressive. White southerners, once overwhelmingly Democratic, shifted to the Republican Party in response to the large though still inadequate gains of the civil rights movement. Men became more Republican, while women remained Democratic. Voters who increasingly identified themselves as religious, including Catholics, became relatively more Republican.[39]

The Republicans, first under Ronald Reagan, then Congressman Newt Gingrich, were able to ride this coalition into the White House in the 1980s and gain control over the House and Senate for three straight terms in the 1990s for the first time since before the 1930s. Yet the Republicans learned that the "Reagan Revolution" did not mean a permanent shift rightward in U.S. politics. The Democrats regained the presidency in 1992 with William Jefferson Clinton, who was reelected in 1996.

Because the president is elected in a nationwide vote while congressmen are elected at the local or state level, there is an incentive for voters to split their vote between parties. The growing distrust of politicians also leads voters to impose a constraint on the federal government by having the legislative and executive branches of government controlled by different parties.[40] President Clinton, consequently, had to deal with a legislature controlled by his opposition, the Republicans.

There are several issues on which President Clinton and the Republicans in Congress saw eye to eye. Trade in particular stands out. But here Clinton had trouble with those in his own party, Democratic congresspeople responding to constituency worries about the loss of jobs and the increasing influence of big corporations, multinationals in particular. The World Trade Organization, globalization meetings, and Most Favored Nation (MFN) status for China are recent examples of the political battles fought over foreign economic policy. China was important for the U.S. economy, and consequently the Clinton administration went all out to convince enough Democratic voters to join with Republicans to secure approval of MFN status.

Despite the importance of examining Democratic and Republican political coalitions, there are several continuities in post–Cold War U.S. foreign policy that are sufficiently strong to merit the label "national consensus." While some voices on the left and right of the U.S. political spectrum may disagree with these policy positions, the constituencies to which politicians of the Democratic and Republican parties look overwhelmingly support these views.

First among these points of foreign policy agreement is the need for the United States to remain engaged in international politics. Although there is an isolationist strain in U.S. foreign policy (generally overblown[41]), it has not dominated in the contemporary period. U.S. actions in the Gulf War, continued participation in NATO and its extension eastward, economic sanctions against Iraq, liberal trade and financial policies, and intervention to defend human rights have all enjoyed popular support.

A second area of consensus concerns the use of military force as a tool of foreign policy. Despite disagreement with many Latin American countries, including Chile, Democratic and Republican constituencies continue to see military force as a legitimate tool in defense of the national interest, however defined. When the use of force is raised, the policy debate within the United States tends to center around its potential costs in U.S. lives and resources.

A final consensus worth highlighting because of its implications for U.S. policy on issues of concern to Latin America, such as drug policy, is the continued view of international politics as a struggle between good and evil. The collapse of communism reinforces the historical view in the United States that its values and policies are the standard-bearers for human progress and dignity. Those who disagree with U.S. policy are assumed to be shortsighted, unenlightened, perhaps even selfish, corrupt, or simply evil.

Conclusion

Domestic politics in Chile and the United States are factors influencing foreign policy. Both countries are democratic, but with institutional structures that reflect the peculiarities of their national experiences. Those institutional structures help us understand the basic continuities in Chilean and U.S. foreign policy despite the end of the Cold War and, in Chile's case, the return of democracy.

Yet a focus on institutional structure is not sufficient to explain continuity in foreign policy. The policy must be implemented in the international arena at costs that are acceptable to constituencies back home. Hence international constraints and opportunities matter. And policy-makers must build a consensus among political actors within their society in favor of those policies. That consensus, however, will also be influenced by a set of actors that have increased in number and diversity in the last thirty years. It is to these transnational actors that we turn in the next chapter.

FOUR

TRANSNATIONAL LINKAGES AND THE BILATERAL RELATIONSHIP

INTERSTATE RELATIONS OFTEN CONTAIN ELEMENTS BEYOND those considered in examining government to government relations. The growth of international interdependence has produced a multitude of nonstate actors engaged in cross-national behavior to influence, regulate, or modify decisions affecting their interests. Nonstate actors, running the gamut from private foreign investors, through missionaries of large religious organizations, to activists of small nongovernmental organizations, are increasingly interacting across national boundaries. Their origins, nature, interests, and objectives differ, in many cases dramatically.

Foreign policy analysis, particularly among states with multiple points of contact in the official and private spheres, needs to consider the impact of these nonstate actors.[1] Most of the early discussions of transnational relations focused on linkages occurring in the economic sphere, where private economic actors attempted to influence decisions by governmental actors. But in the current state of the world, these transnational linkages have spread to encompass more social, cultural, and political realms than in the past.

The resultant and emerging "global civil society" is neither homogeneous nor unified. It reflects the complexities and contradictions introduced by the process of globalization as well as those emerging from domestic civil society itself.

Transnational alliances and societal influences on foreign policy affect the relationship, though less systematically than in the case of international and domestic institutional factors. The impact of the factors examined in this chapter depends heavily upon the issue and context. For example, human rights were very important issues for the transnational alliances in the 1970s but became less so in the 1980s, although the issues continued to be important in Chilean domestic politics.

This chapter analyzes the connections among Chilean and U.S. institutions that are bringing the two countries into a broader range of contact. It consists of two sections. The first section deals with transnational alliances oriented toward influencing policy directly. The subsequent section focuses on society-to-society contacts, in which policy influence is expected to occur indirectly and over a long period of time as a result of cultural contact and the modification of each society's preferences and images of the other resulting from that contact.

Transnational Alliances and the Policy Process

Actors with their own agendas may seek allies outside their country in their efforts to influence national policy. We tend to think of these alliances as occurring among private economic and governmental actors, but in the past few decades there has been a proliferation of "transnational social movement organizations" (TSMOs), whose goals are explicitly political and require globally oriented strategies for their effective implementation. Amnesty International and Greenpeace are representative of this latter form of transnational alliance.[2] The Chile-U.S. relationship is impacted by TSMOs when one government is a target of the movement and the other is pressured to join in the global strategy to bring about the desired change in its behavior. In this section we examine transnational alliances (TNA) in both the economic and human rights arenas, and include TNAs that attempt to influence policy directly or indirectly.

Economic Interests

Private investors from the developed countries have long been the key nongovernmental actors in transnational alliances. But as investors and businesspeople from the developing countries began to engage in business outside their home countries, they too attempted to enlist the aid of the home government to affect policy in the host country that affected their interests.[3]

Chilean foreign investment has grown dramatically in the last two decades. Chile's capital market expanded, deepened, and broadened dramatically in the 1980s as a result of specific government policies and high rates of economic growth. First, the reorganization and privatization of pension funds in 1980 created large institutional investors representing many sectors of Chilean society, including workers. The military government's revised privatization strategies after 1984 subsequently facilitated the growth of these and other investors. The value of stocks transacted increased, in constant U.S. dollars, from $41.9 million in 1984 to $917.6 million in 1989.[4] Consequently, by the end of the 1980s a significant pool of Chilean capital was available for investment, including foreign investment.

As noted in Chapter One (Table 1.4, p. 29), this Chilean capital is invested in neighboring countries, not the United States. Nevertheless, these new Chilean interests increase the likelihood that Chilean private investors, perhaps even including the labor constituency of the socialist and other left parties, will advocate stronger international measures to protect foreign investment. If these policies were to develop, they could put Chile into an alliance with the United States against the wishes of other Latin American countries that are recipients of foreign investment.[5]

After a history of contentious relations between Chile and U.S. foreign investors, relations have generally been very accommodating since Chile's adoption of a neoliberal development strategy. There have been some minor problems affecting foreign investors, particularly in southern Chile, where logging and fish-

TABLE 4.1

State-Owned and State-Managed Enterprises in Selected Years, 1970–1989 (Number of Enterprises)

Enterprises	1970	1973	1983	1989
Enterprises related to CORFO	46	571	24	24
Subsidiaries	46	228	23	24
State-managed	0	325	0	0
Banks	0	18	1	0
Other state-owned enterprises	20	22	21	18
Other financial institutions	2	2	2	2
CODELCO	0	1	1	1
Total	**68**	**596**	**48**	**45**

Notes: CORFO is the State Development Corporation, CODELCO is the National Copper Corporation of Chile.

Source: Adapted from Dominique Hachette and Rolf Luders, *Privatization in Chile. An Economic Appraisal*. San Francisco: International Center for Economic Growth, 1993.

ing multinational corporations (MNCs) have clashed with indigenous groups (Mapuches) and conservationists.

Pinochet's government privatized many of the firms that had been nationalized in the 1960s and before the 1973 coup. Pinochet's nationalism, however, led him to offer full compensation of the value of the companies rather than the actual return (reprivatization) of the copper companies. The democratic governments since 1980 have continued that policy of privatizing many state-owned enterprises (Table 4.1). The state-owned copper company, CODELCO, was not reprivatized and continues as the most important state business in the country and one of the best-run in the world.

U.S. banks and financial institutions have been very active in Chile. Currently there are six such companies in Chile: American Express Bank, Ltd.; Bank of America NT & SA; BankBoston; The Chase Manhattan Bank, NA; Citibank, NA; and the Republic National Bank of New York.[6] Enterprises jointly owned among U.S. and Chilean investors have increased since the return of democracy (Table 4.2).

U.S. companies have developed another route by which to earn money from the Chilean market. In the process, they are making Chilean investors direct partners with an important stake in maintaining good relations with the United States. Franchising is the process by which a firm licenses another investor to utilize its name in selling its product. The new investor pays a fee and gains a recognized name brand and usually extensive training in producing and marketing the product. Table 4.3 lists the U.S. franchises established in Chile; they are nearly all fast-food companies.

The possibility that Chile might join NAFTA provided an opportunity for organized U.S. labor, fearful of a loss of employment in impacted sectors, to make

TABLE 4.2

Enterprises with Both U.S. and Chilean Ownership, 1990–1998

Year	1990	1991	1992	1993	1994	1995	1996	1997	1998	1999
Number of Companies	315	364	420	450	480	500	503	510	512	515

Source: American Chamber of Commerce in Chile. Compiled from the approximate number of firms with Chilean, U.S., Mexican and Canadian ownership.

TABLE 4.3

U.S. Franchises Granted in Chile

Franchise	Sector
Domino's Pizza	Food Service
McDonald's	Food Service
Au Bon Pain	Food Service
Burger King	Food Service
Pizza Hut	Food Service
Taco Bell	Food Service
Kentucky Fried Chicken	Food Service
Alphagraphics	Graphics
Powerhouse Gym	Sporting Goods

Source: U.S. Statistics, 1999, from www.census.gov.

contact with Chilean counterparts also fearful of job loss. During the debate over Mexican accession to NAFTA, U.S. labor was successful in adding provisions to NAFTA on labor and environmental standards that have presumably limited the worst effects of NAFTA on U.S. labor. Chilean and U.S. labor groups initiated talks on common interests but the continued postponement of formal talks by the U.S. government (see chapters Five and Six) diminished the need for strong ties. Labor standards and safeguards, however, will remain a pertinent theme for transnational linkages as long as economic integration remains on the foreign policy agenda.

Among the major Chilean exporters are the fruit growers. "Exports of fruits and vegtables to the US amounted to US$ 524.9 million in 1997. They continue to represent the second most important commodity group in that market. Among the main products exported by Chile to the US are fresh grapes, which account for 14% of total exports, with a total amount of US$ 382 million in 1997."[7] These exports are subject to a series of nontariff barriers in the U.S. such as "marketing orders," purportedly designed to insure a certain level of stability in the market but actually serving to limit imports. Chilean growers are organized into the Federación de Productores de Fruta and the Asociación de Exportadores.

Human Rights

Nongovernmental actors and organizations from the United States actively promote and defend human rights in Chile. Much of the military government's behavior violated U.S. norms, but even under the current democratic regime, U.S. activists remain engaged. This engagement occurs with the acceptance, collaboration, and gratitude of many Chilean NGOs, which are short of the skills and money to influence policy. In addition, they hope in this fashion to add international pressure to domestic efforts to eliminate the authoritarian enclaves discussed in Chapter Three that limit both human rights investigations and democracy.

The heyday of these human rights alliances was the period of the Pinochet dictatorship, when exiled intellectuals, politicians, church people, artists, and musicians traveled and lobbied in the United States advocating a change in United States policy to oppose the junta's violation of human rights, if not overthrow of democracy. Among the more visible of these transnational actors in the United States was Orlando Letelier, Allende's ambassador to the United States who was working with a think tank in Washington, D.C., at the time of his assassination by Pinochet's secret police. Other high-profile Chileans visiting the United States included the musical groups Inti Illimani and Quilapayún, which sang about the violence and horror of the military government. The Letelier type of transnational alliance was designed to affect the U.S. Congress and president directly through research and interest-group politics. The musical groups represented efforts to build a grassroots movement within U.S. society that would then demand the relevant changes in U.S. foreign policy.

Both of these TNAs experienced success in the U.S. Congress and with President Carter, as economic and military sanctions were imposed on the Chilean dictatorship. The human rights TNAs had little direct influence with the Reagan administration. Nevertheless, U.S. Ambassador Harry Barnes played an important role in Chile helping the political opposition gain the political space to contest the referendum on Pinochet and subsequently helping to convince the military to respect the vote for democracy.[8]

In the 1990s the human rights TNAs have been unable to overcome the resistance of the Chilean right wing to accept the constitutional changes that would make the country more democratic. These TNAs had little success with the Clinton administration. The U.S. government resists pressuring the Chilean government to adopt these changes because it recognizes that the Concertación governments lack the necessary institutional and political means to implement rapid and deep changes. Perhaps most important in explaining the decline in the influence of the human rights TNA in bilateral relations is that U.S. society today seems uninterested in organizing around the issue of "authoritarian enclaves," even those that protect violators of human rights (Table 4.4).

There is no counterpart effort on the part of Chilean private citizens and nongovernmental organizations to promote and defend human rights in the United

TABLE 4.4

Chilean NGOs in the Human Rights Arena
Agrupación de Familiares de Detenidos Desaparecidos
Agrupación de Familiares de Ejecutados Políticos
Amnestia Internacional—Chile
CINTRAS—Centro de Salud Mental y Derechos Humanos
CODEJU—Comisiòn de Derechos Juveniles
CODEPU—Corporación de Promoción y Defensa de los Derechos de Pueblo
Comisión Chilena de Derechos Humanos
Corporación de Retornados
Corporación Justicia y Democracia
Corporación Movimiento Anónimo por la Vida
DNI Defensa de los Niños Internacional
Fundación Laura Rodriguez
ILAS—Instituto Latinoamericano de Salud Mental y Derechos Humanos
PIDEE—Fundación de Protección a la Infancia Dañada por los Estados de Emergencia
PRODENI—Corporación Chilena por Derechos de los Niños y de los Jóvenes

States. Certainly there are U.S. official practices that many Chileans see as violating human rights. These include the death penalty in general, and especially that applied to minors, neither of which is practiced in Chile. U.S. immigration policy, especially the increased barriers in the San Diego zone of the Mexican border, which force migrants into the desert and has resulted in over five hundred deaths since their installation in 1995,[9] would also be objectionable to many Chileans. Given Chileans' own concerns about Carabinero violence, they surely must disagree with incidents of police brutality and corruption in a number of major U.S. cities.[10] The recent rise in right-wing and racist vigilantism and mayhem[11] must also appall those Chileans opposed to right-wing violence in their own country.

So why are not Chilean human rights activists pressuring the U.S. government and society on the U.S. human rights record? The answer is probably a combination of too many problems at home (Chile) with which to deal, no money to carry out these campaigns in the United States, and a conviction that U.S. human rights activists will prevail without Chilean aid. There may also be some fear of antagonizing U.S. activists, including those in the U.S. government, who are currently helping Chileans deal with their own human rights abuses.

The result is that the U.S. government and society pressure Chile on human rights issues, but get no pressure in return. The political right in Chile, which resents U.S. official and unofficial pressure in this policy arena, makes isolated references to U.S. human rights abuses but has not engaged in a sustained campaign. More pressing matters at home, a lack of money, and a sense of futility in affecting U.S. policy probably explain the right's general inactivity on this issue in the United States.

Societal Influences on the Bilateral Relationship

Societal influences are more amorphous and diverse than transnational alliances. These influences develop as a result of interactions *per se* and do not require explicit agreements to cooperate in the pursuit of some common goal. Two types of influences at the level of society in general merit attention in this study: cultural exchanges, and environmental activism by private individuals.

Cultural Exchange

In the area of cultural exchanges, relations between Chile and the United States have been less one-sided than in the economic and human rights arenas. Because cultural exchange is influenced by wealth, however, even here the flow of influence is still demonstrably unequal. Migration from Chile to the United States is minor, with little change between the last decade of the military government and the new democratic period. According to the U.S. census, between 1981 and 1991, 23,400 Chileans migrated to the United States, while in the five-year period 1991 to 1996, the total was just under the rate of the prior decade, at 11,400.[12]

Democracy and globalization have made a difference in cultural contact between the two societies in the area of tourism. Eleven airlines from nine countries had flights connecting destinations in the United States and Chile in 1999.[13] In 1985, after the military government had weathered the political crisis created by the 1982 economic collapse, 28,000 tourists visited Chile from the United States. But in the first year of the democratic government, the figure was 54,000 and increased dramatically to 121,000 by 1996.[14] The flow from Chile to the United States also demonstrated a consistent increase throughout the democratic period, as indicated in Table 4.5.

Other means of academic cultural contact include faculty exchanges, dissertations on Chilean topics, and presentations on these topics at professional conferences. The major group of academics focusing on Latin America can be found in the Latin American Studies Association, LASA. At their annual convention in 2000, almost one hundred papers dealing with a Chilean topic were given, and six panels dedicated to Chile alone were held. A number of U.S. universities have developed programs for their undergraduate and graduate students to study in Chile. Some, like Stanford, have established their own campus in Chile, while others, like the University of California and San Diego State University, operate in conjunction with local universities, such as the Universidad de Chile and the Universidad Católica de Chile.

The Chilean education system is among the best in Latin America. Still, many Chileans have historically traveled abroad for advanced degrees. The Chilean government aids these efforts through its scholarship program. Table 4.6 indicates that economics and business administration are the favored fields of study for students receiving these scholarships, followed by other social sciences and natural sciences (see also Table 4.7).

TABLE 4.5

Passengers to the U.S. from Chile 1990–1997

Year	Number
1990	66,300
1991	67,300
1992	76,500
1993	55,800
1994	107,100
1995	122,800
1996	139,100
1997	150,500
Total	**785,400**

Source: "Jefatura de Extranjería y Policía Internacional," Carabineros de Chile, 1998, in *Informe sobre Chile*, Santiago, 1999.

TABLE 4.6

Scholarship Program for Foreign Study*
1990–1998

Field of Study	1990	1991	1992	1993	1994	1995	1996	1997	1998
Economics and Administration	3	5	15	19	16	11	19	15	23
Natural Sciences	6	10	23	9	19	19	19	13	15
Health	6	12	11	13	13	13	27	10	27
Social Sciences and Law	6	10	11	17	16	9	19	16	38
Engineering	5	6	-	5	5	7	12	7	17
Education and Culture	2	5	4	5	6	7	10	6	7
Architecture	1	-	-	1	1	3	3	3	9
Public Administration	-	-	-	-	-	3	7	6	4
Arts	-	-	-	-	-	2	2	4	4
Total	**29**	**48**	**64**	**69**	**76**	**74**	**118**	**80**	**144**

*Number of new scholarships offered each year. Each scholarship supports a program of study that usually extends to 2–3 years.

Source: MIDEPLAN 1998.

TABLE 4.7

Fulbright Exchange Program
Students Studying in Each Country

Year	Chile	USA
1990	35	14
1991	27	25
1992	29	15
1993	27	27
1994	25	21
1995	30	24
1996	36	16
1997	35	21
1998	48	17
1999	37	18

Source: fulcomm@reuna.cl *from email by Jorge Jiménez E., Director Ejecutivo of Fulbright Program in Chile.*

Table 4.8 presents data on the total number of Chileans earning bachelor's, master's and Ph.D. degrees in the United States. These numbers are not restricted to those supported by Chilean government scholarships. Sources of finance for graduate education are limited. The Ford Foundation had a special scholarship program accessed by Chileans from 1991 to 1994, but it was discontinued after awarding a total of fifty-seven fellowships.[15] The U.S. Fulbright Exchange Program also finances student and faculty exchanges.

We can make a rough deduction from a comparison of tables 4.6 (those studying abroad with Chilean government scholarships) and 4.8 (those who have successfully completed their studies in the United States, regardless of source of funding) that most Chileans studying abroad are in countries other than the United States. The dominant degree pursued in the United States is similar to that elsewhere: economics and business administration. But the arts are a close second choice among those studying in the United States, whereas they are among the least supported by Chilean government scholarships.

Religious proselytizing is becoming a major means through which U.S. Protestant culture is penetrating Catholic societies throughout Latin America.[16] Chile has not escaped this phenomenon even as the Catholic Church maintains sufficient political clout to keep Chile the only country in the Americas that does not allow divorce. The Mormon Church has been particularly active in Chile and has experienced attacks by some Chilean nationalists.

One of the greatest means by which cultural exchange is occurring from Chile to the United States is through the literature of Isabel Allende. Initially she

TABLE 4.8

Professional Degrees Granted to Chileans Studying in the United States

Field of Study	1990	1991	1992	1993	1994	1995	1996	1997	1998	1999	Total
Economics and Administration	4	4	2	1	2	6	2	2	-	-	23
Natural Sciences	1	3	2	-	-	-	-	1	-	-	7
Health	1	1	-	1	1	-	-	-	1	-	5
Social Sciences and Law	1	5	3	1	2	3	2	1	-	-	18
Engineering	2	1	3	2	2	-	2	1	1	-	14
Education and Culture	1	5	2	-	3	1	1	-	1	-	14
Architecture	1	-	-	-	-	-	-	-	-	-	1
Public Administration	-	-	-	-	-	1	1	1	-	-	3
Arts	5	1	2	3	-	4	2	-	1	2	20
Total	**16**	**20**	**14**	**8**	**10**	**15**	**10**	**6**	**4**	**2**	**105**

Source: United States Alumni Society, *Directorio*, Santiago, September, 1999.

received attention as the niece of the martyred Salvador Allende, but her writing skills have placed her in the leading group of popular novelists in the contemporary United States. Her novels and memoirs give U.S. readers insights into cultural characteristics such as magical realism and family structure (e.g., *The House of the Spirits* and *Paula*) and Chilean history. Her recent novel, *Daughter of Fortune*, exposes U.S. readers to Chile's European connections (the heroine's adopted mother is English) and historical connections to the United States via Pacific Ocean trade routes, as well as Anglo discrimination against Latin Americans (and other non-Anglos).

Isabel Allende cannot and clearly does not want to escape being a political figure as well. But her message is one of justice and democracy, not revenge. During a reading and book signing at the time that the British were considering extraditing Pinochet to Spain, she was asked to comment on Pinochet's arrest and her feelings about the United States, given its involvement in the coup that deposed and killed her uncle. She responded that Pinochet would not serve a jail term even were he to be extradited, given that Spanish legislation does not permit incarcerating those over seventy-five years of age. As for the United States, she noted that her U.S. audiences did not know what the CIA was currently doing throughout the world and did not know back then. She said she felt very comfortable living in the United States because it was a wonderful country. The applause from the overflow audience was deafening.[17]

Chileans have also made their presence felt among the professorial ranks in U.S. universities. Ariel Dorfmann is a professor of literature at Duke University, author of the award-winning play *Widows*, while his novel *Death and the Maiden* was turned into a movie under the direction of Roman Polanski. Arturo Valenzuela is a professor at Georgetown University and served in the U.S. State Department and National Security Council as well; his brother, Samuel, holds a post at the University of Notre Dame. Other Chileans who stand out are Claudio Grossman, Dean of the Law School at American University, and noted human rights activist Fernando Alegria at Stanford University, and Felipe Aguero at the University of Miami.

Environment

The environment has become an important issue not only within Chile but also between Chile and the United States. The environmental lobby within the United States has proven powerful enough to convince Congress to include environmental issues in any free trade agreement first with Mexico and now with Chile. Internationally oriented NGOs, including those based in the United States, have also been active in protecting the environment in Chile. Most of these are attempts to pressure the government to adopt new policies or enforce legislation already on the books. Yet there are other efforts taking place within the private sector that do not attempt to pressure the national government.

Chile's spectacular Andes Mountains, lakes, and glaciers attract visitors from around the world. One child who loved skiing in Chile in the 1960s grew up to become a multimillionaire, cofounding the Esprit clothing company and investing in The North Face line of adventure clothing and equipment. After selling his share of Esprit in 1990 for an estimated $125 million, Doug Tompkins supported a number of nonprofit ventures, especially ecologically oriented ones. He also began purchasing land in southern Chile, where ancient forests, rare wildlife, and pristine lakes and waterfalls were threatened by the country's rapid free-market development.[18]

In 1991 Tompkins began purchasing land of the *fundo* (ranch) Reñihue in Chile's Region X. Within three years he had amassed 200,000 hectares (1 hectare is equivalent to 2.471 acres) and created El Bosque Pumalín Foundation to administer the lands. Tompkins's strategy seems to have been to quietly work with private individuals and nonprofit groups to develop an apropriate project, then work through the legal and bureaucratic process to set up the nature park.

Tompkins also funded the nonprofit Fundación Educación, Ciencia y Ecología (Educec), run by Chileans and headed by Juan Luis Ysern, bishop of Ancud.[19] Educec petitioned the Honorable Consejo de Monumentos Nacionales de Chile in

April 1995 for a designation as a Natural Sanctuary for 270,000 hectares. Such a designation should have made Tompkins's nonprofit goals clear to everyone. The Consejo's twenty-two members voted unanimously to support the petition with the Minister of Education, who has to sign a decree granting the designation.

Undersecretary of the Interior Belisario Velasco intervened to slow down the process. He argued that the *fundo* Rorohuentro had competing titles for some of the land and that the landholders (*colonos*) on the edge of the proposed sanctuary did not possess clear titles. The bureaucratic process of clarifying land titles seemed bogged down and Educec withdrew its petition after a year in order to bring its properties into clear conformity with the law.

Tompkins continued his self-proclaimed mission while the Pumalín project sputtered. In 1993 and 1994 Tompkins purchased all of the private land (30,000 hectares) in the Melimollo section of Chile's Region XI. The local Melimollo Foundation, purportedly closely tied in with Tompkins, was subsequently enlisted to purchase government-owned land or concessions. Chilean legislation allows for such sales to corporations with well-defined tourism or fish-farming projects. A local historian, however, began a campaign to keep Tompkins from purchasing more land or creating a park in this region as well.

It soon became clear that land titles were not the obstacle for the environmental park. A Christian Democratic senator, Sergio Páez, claimed that Tompkins was part of a foreign conspiracy to depopulate large amounts of land near the Argentine border. These areas would then be impossible to defend. Páez called for the government to repopulate and aid the economic development of these southern regions.[20] Undersecretary Velasco and others denounced Tompkins for allegedly pressuring people into selling their lands. Tompkins was also accused of being against the salmon industry, because he had exposed some of their violations of sanitary and environmental laws. The armed forces were opposed to the park because of the territory's geopolitical significance, and the navy owns land on Huafo Island, rumored to be in Tompkins's future plans.[21]

Tompkins did not lack for allies. Minister of Defense Edmundo Pérez Yoma saw the ecological park as a way to develop these far-flung and scarcely populated territories and therefore decrease their security vulnerabilities.[22] The Environmental Committee of the Chamber of Deputies supported the park. The ecology movement in Chile also came to Tompkins's defense. Alianza por los Bosques, a Chilean NGO, denounced governmental hostility toward the project, as well as dissemination of misinformation. The Instituto de Ecología Política awarded Tompkins its 1995 Earth Alert Award.[23] Richard A. Gephardt, minority leader in the U.S. House of Representatives, called on the executive branch to monitor the Tompkins case when negotiations for Chile's entry into NAFTA began, and U.S. ambassador Gabriel Garcia-Mondragón contacted Chilean authorities about Tompkins's problems.[24]

In 1995 the Chilean government created an Inter-Ministerial Commission, headed by a major figure in the Christian Democratic Party, Genaro Arriagada, to resolve the issue. Tompkins was now insisting on purchasing the 30,000-hectare Huinay *fundo* belonging to the Catholic University of Valparaiso and bifurcating his Pumalín project. The commission supported the park proposal but proposed two alternatives to prevent Tompkins's new purchase. The commission suggested that "the government transfer ownership of the Huinay *fundo* to the nonprofit Education, Science and Technology Foundation, Educec, either directly or by purchasing it first." This was the same foundation that Tompkins wanted to administer the park, but for the commission the benefit lay in the fact that he would then have to apply to Educec for use of the land.[25]

President Frei rejected the commission's proposals. The Interior and Agriculture ministries remained opposed to the project itself, with Undersecretary Velasco demanding to know Tompkins's ultimate goals. Tompkins declared that he was willing to purchase the Huinay *fundo* and turn it over to Educec. There was multiparty support, including by the center-right Renovación Nacional party, in the Chamber of Deputies' Natural Resources, National Properties, and Environmental Commission to accept Tompkins's offer rather than spending U.S. $2 million to buy the *fundo* and transfer it to Educec.[26]

President Frei appointed his chief of staff to negotiate a deal with Tompkins.[27] The agreement was signed on July 7, 1997, over two years after Tompkins had attempted to donate his land for an ecological park. Seven points stand out:[28]

- Tompkins agreed to develop the park and donate the land to a Chilean foundation, while the government agreed to exempt the donation from taxes and designate the park a natural sanctuary.
- Tompkins agreed to cease purchasing more than 4,000 hectares in Regions X and XI until the government could pass legislation regulating land sales.
- The Pumalín Sanctuary would be composed of 250,000 hectares, with another 10,000 hectares for training *colonos* in sustainable means of agriculture.
- Educec was disbanded and a new foundation created to administer Pumalín (subsequently named Fundación Pumalín). The foundation's board of directors would have eight members: four appointed by Tompkins and one each by the Academia de Ciencias de Chile, the Bishopric of Ancud, the Universidad Austral de Valdivia, and, on a six-month rotating basis, a member selected by the local *colonos*. If the project does not come to fruition, the lands will transfer to the university.
- Access through the park will be available for those engaged in productive activities outside the park.

- Mineral and energy prospecting will be allowed within the park.
- Park lands necessary for the construction or maintenance of roads, electrical transmissions, waterways, public beaches, docks, and other uses in the public domain will be granted to the state or relevant third parties.

The effort by Tompkins and Chilean NGOs to work together and present their environmental foes with a fait accompli was significantly watered down in its implementation. But the Tompkins issue was not over yet. The Frei administration pressured the Catholic University of Valparaiso to reject Tompkins's bids and sell its holdings to the Spanish-owned electrical company, Endesa. This corporation intends to build its own park, but not with the ecological emphasis that Tompkins and his Chilean allies favor. Instead, the park will be "the first integral project of sustainable development," a concept that strikes fear into the hearts of ecological activists.[29]

Tompkins continued his activities despite these setbacks. The Frei administration reacted to the Pumalín project by adopting legislation forbidding land purchases by foreigners within five kilometers of the national border. In January 1999 Tompkins purchased 20,000 hectares of native forest bordering on Pumalín Park.

Conclusion

Nonstate actors have become more diverse in the Chile-U.S. relationship. At times the transnational alliances they build make them important actors in the general relationship and may even impact the specific policies that define the bilateral relationship itself.

U.S. nonstate actors bring resources that are scarce in Chile (money and organizational expertise) to influence Chile's polity and society. Chilean nonstate actors use different resources to have impact in the United States. One of the major voices in exile, Inti Illimani, combines Chilean, World Music, and other musical traditions in its rendition of Andean music; and Isabel Allende imbues her fiction with a strong dose of Chilean culture.

The Tompkins episode suggests a limit to the influence of transnational relations built on society-to-society relations. Those interactions ultimately take place in a context defined and regulated by the state. Tompkins and his allies believed that they could simply outmaneuver their adversaries in the environmental arena. But on a politicized issue their opponents found political space and opportunity to pressure the government into intervening in what should have been merely a private-sector transaction, which subsequently followed the legally defined path to its goal.

In summary, transnational relations need to be placed in their domestic context to be understood. And ultimately, the international opportunities and constraints that governments face in making policy will affect their impact. With these conclusions, we are now ready to analyze Chilean-U.S. relations over the period of the two democratic governments in the 1990s.

THE MATURING (?) OF THE CHILEAN–UNITED STATES RELATIONSHIP

FIVE

REESTABLISHING COOPERATIVE RELATIONS: THE AYLWIN ADMINISTRATION

COOPERATIVE RELATIONS REQUIRE MORE THAN GOODWILL, because cooperation implies adjusting one's policies to accommodate at least some of the interests of the other actor. In addition, given the dramatic international and domestic changes that occurred in the 1980s, new issues on which Chile and the United States would not see eye to eye were bound to emerge.

This chapter examines the efforts of the Aylwin administration (1990–1994) to cooperate with the United States to an extent beyond what had been accomplished even in the days of the Alliance for Progress. The administration's interlocutors in the Bush and Clinton administrations held similar views. As noted in Chapter Two, asymmetries in the relationship's meaning to each country remained, with the United States of more interest to Chile than vice versa.

For the United States, Chile was one of many countries in the Western Hemisphere, and certainly not as important as Mexico or Brazil. The region itself lagged behind Europe and Asia in priority. The United States wanted to build a new world order for the post–Cold War. Democracy, free trade, and free movement of capital would be the pillars of the new world order, and the United States would patrol it, in conjunction with the UN Security Council when possible, unilaterally when necessary. Chile was a small cog in this scenario, useful because of its success with economic reform and redemocratization, but still a small cog.

The institutional and coalitional characteristics of Chile's redemocratization, analyzed in Chapter Three, provided the domestic context for Chile's foreign policy. Aylwin wanted to use foreign relations to buttress democracy at home by building up international support for the Concertación government and producing economic growth to fuel a broader-based national development. For Chile, the United States was one of multiple areas of interest as the country sought reinsertion into the international community after seventeen years of pariah status. The United States could potentially offer important economic and diplomatic benefits for Chile. Aylwin's challenge with respect to relations with the United States was basically to meet U.S. requirements for better relations without simply allowing the United States to determine Chilean foreign policy.

Aylwin had to meet some U.S. demands because many of the sanctions the United States had imposed on the military government did not go away by virtue of a new government assuming office. In addition, the United States was not happy with the "authoritarian enclaves" that gave the military protection and independence vis-à-vis the civilian government. (It had fewer qualms about the voting procedures that increased minority parties' influence in the legislature.) So the United States was not willing to drop charges and demands and begin with a clean slate.

Chileans of all political stripes were anxious to see how relations would develop. Both the left and right hoped that the United States could avoid the temptation of imposing political conditions that responded to U.S. rather than Chilean political conditions. For the right, the United States would avoid discussions of authoritarian enclaves and political legacies of the military regime, and instead focus on the economic inheritance of the new government. On the left, there was a desire to gain U.S. support for human rights and democracy in Chile. The Aylwin government would need to demonstrate that the era of "frank cooperation" with the United States could be beneficial to Chile.[1]

In this chapter we analyze the Aylwin administration's successes in putting the bilateral relationship on a footing of greater cooperation than ever before. We also examine those areas in which progress was too slow to reach resolution during these four years. The major areas examined are military and economic relations, along with two minor issues on the agenda: narcotrafficking and extradition. In the conclusion we discuss how international, domestic, and transnational factors combined to produce this new beginning for the bilateral relationship.

Military Relations

Aylwin needed to establish a good working relationship with the armed forces, given their influence as a result of the 1980 Constitution. The navy and air force were receptive, but with Pinochet back as commander in chief of the army, relations were difficult. A good working relationship would require not only that the armed forces focus on nonpolitical missions, but also that they receive the equipment and training necessary for those missions.

Since the United States had limited many bilateral military contacts, reestablishing normal relations in the military arena offered benefits for both the Aylwin administration and the armed forces. For the government, lifting these restrictions would be one more signal to the international community (including investors) that Chile was no longer a pariah state. In addition, the Aylwin administration could lay claim with its armed forces to opening up possibilities for equipment and training in the United States. Chile's armed forces were certainly interested in maintenance and new equipment as well as increased training opportunities.

Aylwin's administration moved quickly to improve relations in this area. The major outstanding issue was the Kennedy embargo. The chief obstacle to lifting the embargo lay in making progress on the Letelier case. There were two aspects with which to deal. A civil suit had been filed in U.S. federal court for "wrongful death" damages against the Chilean government in 1978, and in 1980 the Chilean government had been found liable. Pinochet's government refused to accept the ruling and continued to obstruct investigation of the criminal case in the United States.

The first step for Aylwin's government was to deal with the issue of damages. In 1989 the United States had proposed submitting a proposal for compensation of the Letelier and Moffit families to a commission of jurists under the Bryan-Suárez Mújica treaty of 1916 between Chile and the United States. In his first month in office, Aylwin agreed and submitted the proposal to Congress for approval. The right denounced the arbitration as tantamount to admitting guilt before a trial had established criminal responsibility.[2] Yet during the secret vote in January 1991, some appointed senators apparently favored arbitration, because the proposal passed. (One can speculate that these would have included the military appointees, given the nature of the Kennedy sanctions.) In addition, and as part of a larger package to deal with political-prisoner cases, the Minister of Justice was able to get the Letelier case transferred out of military courts and appoint a special investigating judge to handle the case in July, 1991.[3]

Although it would take at least a year to make significant progress, the Bush administration demonstrated its willingness to move quickly on these two issues. There was a flurry of activity associated with Defense Minister Patricio Rojas's trip to Washington in March 1991. Chile received a number of benefits from the visit. Undersecretary of Defense for Latin America Nancy Dorn testified before the House Foreign Affairs Committee that Chile would receive $1.1 million in military aid for 1992.[4] Rojas signed a broad-ranging agreement with the Pentagon. In the strictly military realm, Chile was provided with aid for "education, training, logistics and operations" as well as being reincorporated into the Foreign Military Sales program. A public declaration by the U.S. government that civilians were indispensable participants in the defense arena was useful in the civil-military debate at home. Upon returning home, Minister Rojas also highlighted that, unlike previous agreements, this one excluded aid for internal order and security because they lay outside the bounds of the defense arena.[5] The Chilean and U.S. Air Force chiefs also met that March to normalize relations between the two service branches.[6]

The fruits of this new cooperation on defense were not long in ripening. Within a week, the Chilean Navy had invited Admiral Alfred Gray to visit in April; the U.S. Navy would also send a team to evaluate the needs and requirements of the Chilean Navy. The next day the Chilean Air Force announced the purchase of two Hercules C-130 transport planes. In May 1991, Minister Rojas, Chilean Ambassador to the U.S. Patricio Silva, U.S. Colonel Wayne Erwin, and the commercial attache of the U.S. Embassy in Chile met to establish the channels for Chilean purchases. The first contract was signed in August between the Empresa

Nacional de Aeronaútica (ENAER) and General Electric for parts for two combat fighters. Joint exercises were also expanded.[7]

Bilateral military relations reflected some of the tensions in Chilean civil-military relations. As noted in Chapter Three, the air force and navy were attempting to accommodate themselves to the new political situation by focusing on their military missions. Consequently, there was a great deal of interaction with their U.S. counterparts. The army, on the other hand, was mired in defending its prerogatives and the authoritarian enclaves in the political system. Both of these goals were directly contrary to U.S. efforts to consolidate a liberal democracy and civilian control over the military, and are partly reflected in the low level of contact between the two armies.

Just as relations were improving in the defense arena, a major controversy was narrowly averted. In late 1991, the U.S. Congress debated a foreign assistance bill proposing that sales to some countries, Chile included, require the executive to provide Congress with fifteen days notice of the value and purpose of any transfer of military resources. In Chile the right became concerned that such a stipulation not only singled out Chile but also could constitute a new attempt to use military relations to pressure Chile on civil-military reform. Members of Renovación Nacional demanded that Ambassador Guillespie clarify why Argentina, Bolivia, and Peru were not included in the list. The ambassador attempted to explain that this was a subject of legislative-executive relations within the United States, and that Israel and Egypt were also subject to such considerations. But the right would not be silenced until Congress dropped the provision in its final version of the bill.[8]

A minor controversy erupted in 1992 that brought protests from both the right and left in Chile. A Chilean arms manufacturer, Carlos Cardoen, flaunted various international arms embargoes by selling cluster bombs. In March 1992, U.S. customs seized one of his helicopters in transit in Dallas, on the grounds that its sale violated U.S. export permits for some of its parts. Cardoen attempted to get Chile's government to intervene on his behalf, but the Ministry of Foreign Affairs saw the dispute as a private matter and refused. The entrepreneur presented his case to Chile's Congress. The right immediately came to Cardoen's defense, alleging that the craft was for civilian use and that the United States did not want the economic competition. But Socialist Party Senator Ricardo Nuñez also found a U.S. embargo on any Chilean product "unacceptable," and a deputy from the Christian Democrats called it an "abusive situation." The government, nevertheless, was not forced to backtrack and defend the Chilean businessman. The issue seemed to resolve itself when Cardoen won his case in U.S. court.[9]

Unfortunately, this minor irritant would not go away. Although the U.S. government lost in the helicopter case, it subsequently sought Cardoen's extradition for violating U.S. export controls to Iraq.[10] This time Aylwin's administration immediately undertook his defense, but Aylwin would leave office with the case still pending.

Economic Relations

In the economic arena, the major issue throughout the Aylwin administration was the question of a free-trade agreement with the United States. Unfortunately, neither this issue nor the poisoned grapes or intellectual property rights cases would be solved, and they continued to produce strains in the relationship, especially among the Chilean right. Other economic issues on the agenda more successfully addressed were the Generalized System of Preferences (GSP) and the Overseas Private Investment Corporation (OPIC) insurance.

Free-Trade Agreement

President Bush announced a new orientation in U.S. policy toward the hemisphere a few months after Aylwin assumed office in Chile. The Enterprise Initiative for the Americas proposed that an association of states "from Alaska to Antartica" be created. The basis for the association would be free trade, private investment, and economic growth. For those countries with debt problems, new mechanisms would be developed to relieve the debt burden.[11]

The United States recognized that few countries in the hemisphere had the requisite economic structure and stability to enter into such an association. In order to prepare countries for the negotiations to create the association, the United States proposed the adoption of framework agreements. (As executive agreements, they do not require Congressional approval as does an actual free-trade agreement; see Chapter Three.) The Bush administration also committed itself to the creation of a multilateral fund to facilitate market liberalization and private investment. In addition, a new stimulus to debt reduction was added to the Brady Plan: it would now be possible to reduce debt owed to the U.S. government via debt-for-environment swaps.

The Aylwin government was delighted with the initiative. Chile had already undergone the necessary structural economic reforms and it hoped that joining an association with the United States would alleviate some of the other trade issues on the bilateral agenda. Aylwin encountered no opposition in principle from the right in Chile. The right was anxious for the economy to enjoy the benefits of the initiative. In addition, right-wingers believed that U.S. eagerness for a treaty would produce a more favorable negotiating context for Chile.[12]

The Aylwin administration had to make a foreign policy choice before approaching the United States. Upon taking office, the new democratic government made relations with other Latin American countries a priority. To wait, however, for its neighbors to undertake the requisite structural economic adjustments and then negotiate as a group with the United States might take years. The need of the Concertación development program to produce wealth to distribute (see Chapter Three) also augured for a quick decision. Aylwin consequently opted for a unilateral approach to the Initiative for the Americas. Finance Minister Alejandro Foxley traveled to Washington two weeks after Bush's announcement to proclaim Chile's agreement with the initiative and desire to develop a framework agreement.

Aylwin's decision encountered little opposition at home, where most economic sectors saw an agreement as positive for the country but not especially for themselves. The country's largest exporters (minerals firms, especially those in copper) did little business in the United States and focused on Asia Pacific for the future. Fisheries faced no trade barriers in the U.S. market. Both sectors believed that an agreement might have benefits for them over a longer term if investors were attracted. Fisheries thought that perhaps an ability to export higher-value-added products (i.e., processed fish) might stimulate domestic producers and that perhaps technology costs might decrease. Environmental protection was not yet an issue in 1991, though it would become so later.[13] Labor, still handcuffed by the Pinochet-era labor laws, knew that it could not successfully oppose an agreement and sought to influence the terms instead.[14]

Members of the Confederación de la Producción y del Comercio (CPC), largely industrialists and agroindustrialists, were excited by the prospect of a free-trade agreement with the United States. For many of these businesspeople, the small size of the internal market meant that sales growth would best come from international markets, and the U.S. market was huge and rich. An agreement would help those products not included in the GSP, would reduce tariffs, should eliminate tariffs that varied according to U.S. production cycles (such as in dehydrated onions), and would attract foreign investment. Some entrepreneurs even thought that greater access to the U.S. market would help Chile negotiate greater access to the European and Asian markets. They did not expect a large influx of U.S. goods and thought that in those areas where adjustment costs were high, the agreement should be phased in over time.[15]

President Bush, and later Clinton, had good intentions in proposing a free-trade agreement with Chile. But Congress would have to approve any agreement, and there the prospects were not very good. The Democrats controlled the House, and the Chairman of the Ways and Means Committee Dan Rostenkowski had a competing trade bill. The economy was in recession, and the political calendar promised an election-year fight on free trade.[16] Candidate Clinton attacked NAFTA, although he would later support it as president. After a strenuous battle over Mexican accession to NAFTA in the first half of the Clinton administration, there were not enough congressional votes to incorporate Chile, even if arrangements could have been made to meet Congress's demands on labor and environmental issues.

U.S. Undersecretary of the Treasury Davis Mulford visited Santiago in August 1990 to begin negotiations. The negotiations moved quickly with Chile's Finance, rather than Foreign Affairs, Ministry taking the lead. In October, during President Aylwin's visit to Washington, the Framework Agreement was signed. A Bilateral Council for Trade and Investment was created to begin informally studying the economic issues involved in negotiating a free-trade agreement. A dispute mechanism for trade and investment issues was established. An annex called for cooperation between the two countries at the GATT multilateral negotiations; developing mechanisms to reduce barriers to trade and investment; increased access to markets for goods and services; and the protection of intellectual property rights.

While Chile was interested in moving quickly, the first priority for the Bush administration was to move ahead with global GATT negotiations and then a bilateral agreement with Mexico. After Mexico, there was a preference for negotiating with groups of countries, because negotiation and implementation would be more efficient.[17]

In March 1991 Bush asked Congress to extend his negotiating authority under fast-track legislation. He mentioned that Chile would be among the potential parties with whom the United States would negotiate a free-trade agreement. The Aylwin administration took the explicit mention of Chile as a good sign, and Finance Minister Alejandro Foxley publicly declared that negotiations could be completed by October, with an agreement signed in November of 1991.[18]

But in November, Minister Foxley could only make a joint announcement with Special Trade Representative Carla Hills that both countries were interested in moving forward on a free-trade agreement. In early 1992, the United States agreed to transfer interest on Chile's official debt to the United States for financing of environmental protection projects. Since any likely free-trade agreement progress would include environmental stipulations, this move represented more progress in Chilean eyes.

In April 1992, just before Aylwin's second visit to Washington, Ambassador Curtis Kamman presented the issues that the United States wanted addressed in a free-trade agreement. These were: 1) gradual reduction of tariffs on all trade; 2) gradual reduction of nontariff barriers; 3) increased market access for services; 4) the establishment of norms providing foreign investors with treatment equivalent to that provided national investors, and the elimination of restrictions on investments; 5) adequate protection for intellectual property, patents, and trademarks; 6) special regulations for trade in natural resources and related products; 7) technical and country-of-origin regulations, public health requirements, exclusions for reasons of national security, and dispute mechanisms; 8) penalties for government policies such as subsidies, foreign exchange controls, restrictions, and so on.[19]

Progress on an agreement, however, was being derailed in Washington. Not only was the NAFTA struggle in Congress dominating the executive's attention, but Chile's position was losing out in the bureaucratic struggles within the executive branch. The major advocate for a treaty with Chile was the Treasury Department. For Treasury, Chile deserved a reward for its leadership in economic reform in the region. In addition, and like the Aylwin administration itself, Treasury saw a free-trade treaty primarily in terms of its impact on private financial flows. But the Office of the U.S. Trade Representative (USTR), with the Commerce Department as an ally, focused on trade. In general USTR preferred to negotiate with a group of countries in Latin America and it was unimpressed by Chile's rank as thirty-eighth trade partner of the United States.[20] The environmental NGO, Defenders of Wildlife, petitioned for a halt to crab imports from Chile for allegedly killings thousands of dolphins, seals, and other marine mammals for bait.[21] Given the importance of environmental issues in the NAFTA negotiations, this charge further undermined Chile's position.

When Aylwin met Bush in May, the U.S. president said the right things from a Chilean perspective. In a South Lawn press conference at the White House, Bush praised Chile, saying: "Today Chile gives hope to an entire hemisphere. With market-oriented reforms, you've led by example."[22] But with the decision to put Chilean negotiations behind Mexico, a free-trade agreement was effectively precluded during Aylwin's tenure.

There was bipartisan disagreement in Chile in evaluating the Aylwin trip. Even before the trip, Senator Sebastian Piñera (RN) had noted with cynicism that the United States, which declared itself the champion of free trade, had yet to sign such an agreement with any Latin American country. The President of the Confederación de la Producción y el Comercio expressed disappointment at the postponement. Former presidential candidate Francisco Javier Errázuriz said the trip was a mistake and actually represented a step back in the relationship. The Instituto Libertad, closely linked to Pinochet, called the trip a failure because important issues, such as U.S. trade barriers and the poisoned grapes case, were not even discussed. Concertación member Senator Laura Soto (Partido por la Democracia) accused the U.S. government of deflating the country's hopes and called on the government to look more closely at relations with the rapidly growing Asian economies.[23]

Some politicians on the right found benefits in the trip. UDI Senator Beltrán Urenda called the trip a success, but attributed it to the prestige of the country (presumably the result of Pinochet's "successes"). RN Senator Miguel Otero said the Bush commitment was more than might have been expected, "given the political climate in the U.S." The private sector was also stimulated by the visit. The American Chamber of Commerce in Chile created a Council of Free Trade between Chile and the U.S.[24]

President Bush's formal announcement that Chile would be next in line after Mexico was generally well received by the Concertación parties in Chile. While disappointed, these parties expected to continue in office after Aylwin's tenure ended in early 1994. They took heart in Bush's commitment to pursue an agreement later, but most of all in the reputational benefits generated by the trip. Economics Minister Carlos Ominami noted that the trip produced three concrete results. The United States committed itself at the highest levels of government to begin negotiations with Chile at some point in the future and praised Chile for its successful democratic transition and economic policies. As a result, positive signals about Chile's future were sent to the international financial community. Foreign Minister Enrique Silva Cimma expressed similar sentiments, and Treasury Minister Foxley said U.S.-Chilean relations were at their most cooperative level ever.[25]

Poisoned Grapes

Chilean society and politicians were largely united behind producers' demands that the U.S. government provide some compensation to Chile. There was a feeling that the United States had "overreacted" when two grapes out of millions were discovered with small amounts of cyanide. In addition, Chilean courts and a congressional committee established that poisoning the grapes could not have occurred in Chile and therefore occurred in the United States itself. The right in Congress also pointed out, in the discussions on submitting the Letelier civil case to the Bryan-Suárez Mújica commission (see below), that the United States should make a similar gesture in the grapes case.[26]

In January 1991, the Aylwin administration presented a formal complaint against the U.S. Food and Drug Administration (FDA) for its behavior in the grapes case. Foreign Minister Silva Cimma declared that Chile's government would exhaust all means necessary to ensure that justice was achieved. He also noted that the U.S. government should be responsible for damages caused by the errors committed by members of its bureaucracy. Minister Silva Cimma noted that Chile would try to resolve this issue through bilateral negotiations, but that if they failed, Chile would invoke the Bryan-Suárez Mújica treaty to create a commission that would establish the facts of the case.[27]

Chilean producers had gone to court seeking damages, but their first attempt proved futile. Ambassador Kamman commented that the U.S. government did not believe that it was liable for damages caused by the grape embargo. He also noted that Chile's efforts to utilize the Bryan-Suárez Mújica treaty would pose bilateral problems, because the parties were not obligated to accept its jurisdiction on a particular matter. Kamman was satisfied that the United States had not acted negligently and had met its responsibility.[28]

After a U.S. federal judge exonerated the FDA from damages, President Aylwin sent the matter to his Consejo de Defensa del Estado (not to be confused with the National Security Council) in January 1993. The Chamber of Deputies and Senate responded by asking the president to invoke the Bryan-Suárez Mújica treaty, as did the Minister of Agriculture. Foreign Minister Silva Cimma and Government Minister Enrique Correa, however, counseled continuing direct bilateral discussions. The Chamber of Deputies continued to pressure Aylwin by formally presenting the Foreign Ministry with its earlier report concluding that the grapes had not been poisoned in Chile.[29] But, to the dismay of the exporters, Aylwin decided to continue trying to resolve the issue via bilateral diplomacy.[30]

Within a week, however, Aylwin gave in to the domestic pressure for resolving the issue. His ambassador to the United States contributed to turning up the heat at home. The ambassador publically declared that the Pinochet government had compensated 94 percent of the producers' losses.[31] Chile's government now formally requested that a commission under the Bryan-Suárez Mújica treaty review the issue. The new Clinton administration, however, refused to invoke the treaty and suggested the creation of a bilateral commission to resolve the issue. There was little the Aylwin administration could do but accept the U.S. offer.[32] The issue dragged on from there, leaving a solution to be negotiated by the next Chilean administration.

Intellectual Property Rights

Closely related to the free-trade issue but separate from it was the issue of intellectual property rights, particularly as they affected pharmaceuticals. This was not only an issue of Chilean legislation; the United States brought up the topic as a general issue in the GATT global negotiations. But Chile could not escape direct pressure. The U.S. pharmaceutical industry threatened to oppose a free-trade agreement if Chilean legislation was not modified.[33]

The left and right in Chile were united in opposing U.S. efforts in this area without some concrete benefits from the United States. They felt that Chile had already made concessions in submitting the grapes case to a bilateral commission as an alternative to the Bryan-Suárez Mújica treaty. The lack of reciprocity led Socialist Deputy Jaime Naranjo to call for a suspension in the work of the bilateral commission. The U.S. allegation that Cardoen had violated U.S. patents in the helicopter case discussed above also produced bipartisan critiques of U.S. behavior.

Neither the Bush nor Clinton administrations wished to wait for a free-trade agreement in order to address the issue. On a trip to Chile, a Commerce Department official, Myles Frechette, announced that the United States wanted to negotiate on intellectual property rights and investment legislation *before* a free-trade treaty. Although Minister of the Economy Onimani insisted that Chile would only negotiate a package deal, congressional sources in the United States insisted that the free-trade agreement would proceed more easily if there were already agreements on these two matters.[34]

Chile fared no better on this point with the change in administration in the United States. Shortly after taking office, Clinton sent a letter to Aylwin indicating that he supported the idea of a free-trade agreement with Chile but wanted to start bilateral negotiations on intellectual property rights and investment.[35]

OPIC, GSP

Chile was suspended in 1987 from the Generalized System of Preference (GSP) and Overseas Private Investment Corporation (OPIC) insurance systems because of the military government's repressive labor legislation.[36] With the return of democracy, Congress quickly modified the labor legislation and the Aylwin administration asked the U.S. Department of Commerce for reinstatement into the programs. During President Bush's visit to Chile in December 1990 (the first by a U.S. president in thirty years), he announced that Chile would be included in both programs. But the U.S. bureaucracy was apparently "busy," and Bush had other priorities. Chileans were aggravated by the delays. At the end of January, the Chilean Chamber of Deputies complained to the Foreign Ministry, and the president of the Senate traveled to Washington to investigate. Finally, on February 5, 1991, President Bush signed the official decree.[37]

Other Issues on the Agenda

Narcotrafficking

Chile is not a major player in the international political economy of drugs, and both governments were keen to keep it that way. The major issues were the possibility of alternative transportation routes through northern Chile (which borders on Bolivia and Peru, the chief coca-growing countries) and money laundering through the nation's financial system. Some military cooperation was entered into.[38] But given the nature of the drug issue in Chile, militarization of its drug policy was not likely. Consequently, Chile had very good relations on the drug issue during the Aylwin administration.

The Interior minister sought U.S. training to help Chilean police deal with drug trafficking, money laundering, and terrorism. He also asked the FBI to open an office in Chile for such training. Faced with concerns by politicians within the Concertación, Minister Krauss clarified that FBI agents would only assist in training and not engage in any intelligence gathering. The U.S. Drug Enforcement Agency (DEA) helped train the Carabineros, but again without taking an active role. Although denounced by the right for allowing foreigners into Chile's police institutions, the Aylwin administration continued the programs.[39] The U.S. Ambassador also played an important role in Chilean Congressional debates on a new drug law.[40]

Extradition

The Aylwin administration was appalled by the decision of the U.S. Supreme Court that it was not a violation of U.S. laws to kidnap someone in another country in order to bring him or her to trial in the United States. President Aylwin himself noted that the decision appeared contrary to international law. Although U.S. Ambassador Kamman noted that Chile was not affected by the decision because justice could be applied in the country, Minister Krauss not only rejected the ruling, but said that Chile would prevent any such actions on national territory.[41]

The Aylwin government enjoyed the full support of the right, which characterized the U.S. decision as an attack on international law because it privileged the use of force above the law.[42] It is probably the case that the right worried that some Chileans might be subject to such measures, because the Chilean courts cannot prosecute most human rights crimes as a result of the 1978 amnesty.

Conclusion

The bilateral agenda in 1990 was dominated by the legacy of seventeen years of military rule with an abundance of human rights abuses, both in Chile and internationally. The international and domestic transformations discussed in chapters Two and Four provided an opportunity to improve dramatically the bilateral relationship.

Patricio Aylwin's administration tackled these major problems head-on. Creating a new relationship largely depended upon the new Chilean government recognizing the inherent asymmetries between the two countries. Chile adjusted more than the United States, because the U.S. government was willing to budge very little from its preferred policies. The U.S. Congress had its own agenda for the relationship, but even the Clinton administration wanted something (protection for intellectual property) although it could not deliver something else (a free-trade agreement).

Aylwin and the Concertación were willing to accept this asymmetric basis for developing new relations for three major reasons having to do with domestic politics and international finance. First, giving in on some things helped them in political battles at home (i.e., the leftover issues with the military government). Second, because the United States did not say "no" outright to anything Chile wanted, there was always hope that further negotiations could produce a better deal (e.g., on grapes). Finally, the Aylwin administration was willing to accept these terms because the most important benefit it believed it could get from the United States was a reputational one. A good relationship with the United States would be a signal to foreign investors that Chile was the place to be and a signal to the right at home that democracy was the only way to go.

It would be up to the Frei administration to discover whether this situation could continue to be in Chile's interest once it had consolidated its new reputation.

SIX

A MATURING OF THE RELATIONSHIP?

WHEN EDUARDO FREI RUIZ-TAGLE ASSUMED OFFICE IN 1994, Chile's democracy took a major step toward consolidation. Not only had another election been held cleanly; the center-left coalition's victory was respected by the military and the political right. The system designed by Pinochet and his handpicked advisors in 1980 had worked: the people's voice had been heard at the ballot box, but the institutional constraints of the constitution had limited the scope of change that a reformist government could implement.

The bilateral relationship with the United States had improved dramatically over the prior four years. Goodwill and common interests could be found across the entire gamut of relations on both sides. Frei's agenda for relations with the United States contained some issues still unresolved after Aylwin's tenure as well as a number of new issues.

Chief among the holdover issues were the poisoned grapes case and free-trade negotiations. The accession of Chile to the North American Free Trade Agreement (NAFTA) was especially important because it was perceived by Chile to be a means of consolidating the country's diverse economic and political relations. Chief among the new issues was an accusation of dumping brought against Chilean salmon. This product was a new and highly successful Chilean export, and thus the case caused the government and entrepreneurs to worry that protectionist measures in key markets could limit Chile's development model.

This chapter consists of three substantive sections and a conclusion. We first examine the evolution of bilateral relations in the security realm. Both countries had multiple common interests ranging from promoting transparency and confidence-building measures among Latin American rivals, to keeping the arms bazaar open to Latin America. Cooperation was consequently easier to achieve in this sphere than in the economic one. Points of friction did arise, but they were on issues that, given the new international and regional context, turned out to be quite minor. Our second section examines human rights issues, chiefly the international and Chilean efforts to hold General Pinochet accountable despite the amnesty passed by the military government. The United States was very accommodating to the interests of the Frei government, supporting Chilean efforts to prevent Pinochet from facing trial outside Chile but also supporting efforts to bring him to trial within Chile. A third section focuses on economic relations. The cases of poisoned grapes, salmon dumping, and the failure to gain access to

NAFTA became contentious at times and demonstrate both the possibilities and limits to the relationship.

Our conclusion summarizes how international, domestic, and transnational factors facilitate the pursuit of cooperative relations even in the face of setbacks on specific issues. The future looks promising for this relationship partly because the international context is constraining upon Chile but not so much that the Concertación's domestic political and economic needs cannot be met. Just as importantly, the international context is such that even when U.S. domestic politics produce outcomes detrimental to Chile, they do not foreclose cooperation on other matters of mutual interest.

Security Relations

Chile and the United States created a High Level Consultation Mechanism in 1994 that covered security matters. On July 16, 1996 the Chilean and U.S. defense ministers signed a Memorandum of Cooperation on Defense and Security Matters to build on that initial effort. The countries agreed to establish a Consultative Committee on Defense that would: 1) institutionalize a process of consultations on defense and security matters; 2) establish a working agenda that would broaden cooperative efforts; and 3) develop a conceptual framework to strengthen confidence between the two defense establishments.

Meetings were to be held at least once a year. Specific committees would be established as required by the policy and technical issues before the Consultative Committee. Three subcommittees were initially created: a Committee on Military Cooperation, a Committee for the Formation of Civilian Experts in the Area of Defense, and a Committee on Science and Technology.

This memorandum of understanding has permitted a greater sense of closeness and cooperation between the two countries. Evidence of this spirit can be found at the hemispheric meetings of defense ministers, particularly the 1996 meeting held in Bariloche, Argentina. At that meeting, Chile supported the initiative of the U.S. secretary of defense for the creation of a center for hemispheric defense studies. Cooperation is also evident in the OAS on the need to develop and strengthen confidence-building measures in the hemisphere.

U.S. Ambassador to Chile John O'Leary recently summed up bilateral security relations as follows:

> The focus of our bilateral defense interactions is orchestrated in response to the Theater Engagement Program (TEP) elaborated by the U.S. Southern Command. General Wilhelm of the U.S. Southern Command and his staff, including the members of our U.S. Military Group in Santiago, have responded to the mandate of the U.S. National Military Strategy (to shape the security environment, respond as necessary to challenges, and prepare for an uncertain future) by building an engagement plan entitled Cooperative Regional Peacetime Engagement.

> Of course, we have had a great deal more military-to-military contact. In fact, $450,000 in International Military Education and Training (IMET) funds have facilitated the attendance of Chilean military personnel in our war colleges, in technical training, in resource management courses, even in orientation courses at Fort Benning, Georgia for the entire senior year class of the Escuela Militar. The funds provided by General Wilhelm for professional interchange, known as Traditional Commander in Chief Activities (TCA) funds—this year totaling nearly $900,000—have facilitated interactions both here in Chile and in the U.S. that run the spectrum from observation of a major air defense exercise called Roving Sands to the deployment of over 250 U.S. Air Force personnel and ten aircrafts to the FIDAE air show. One of the most important interactions is the Washington Studies trip taken by ANEPE in the August-to-October time frame. . . . [1]

Military relations were extremely cooperative, as Frei's Defense Ministry reaped the benefits of Aylwin's success in eliminating most of the restrictions on bilateral contact in this policy arena. Joint maneuvers reached a new level when Chile was the only Latin American nation to participate in RIMPAC '96, the war games held off Hawaii's coast. For ten days, forty warships, three hundred combat planes, and thirty thousand soldiers from six nations (the United States, Australia, Canada, Japan, South Korea, and Chile) played with more firepower "clustered within a few hundred square miles of ocean than during all of World War II."[2] Chile was also the first Latin American country to publish a defense white paper. Both the United States and Chile have encouraged such policy statements throughout the region as a contribution to consolidating peaceful relations.

The two countries also found common interests in the arms markets, where the United States is a seller and Chile a buyer. The U.S. government is the largest arms exporter in the world. President Carter halted the export of sophisticated weaponry to Latin America, and Presidents Reagan and Bush continued that ban. Chile's military modernization program stimulated a reevaluation of U.S. arms export policy to the region. Clinton's defense secretary, William J. Perry, raised the issue of the ban in 1996. He argued that Latin America was treated differently from countries elsewhere in the world, where sales were evaluated on a case-by-case basis. Perry also joined with the U.S. arms industry in arguing that Latin American arms purchases in Europe meant fewer jobs for U.S. labor.[3] In order to compete for the Chilean order for twenty to twenty-four advanced fighter jets (worth more than $400 million), the Clinton administration decided in August 1997 to lift the arms ban.[4]

Chile's military modernization programs enjoy guaranteed funding via the copper provision in the constitution. Chile purchased some less-sophisticated military aircraft from the United States and Belgium, then sought more sophisticated and new weaponry. But the new purchases ran into difficulty at home with the onset of recession. During the 1999 presidential campaign the candidates of the Concertación and the right asked President Frei to allow the incoming government to decide how much will be spent on the air force's modernization. Whether the United States would get the contract, however, is unclear. Some Chileans still worry about the reliability of the United States as an arms supplier and would prefer to purchase the planes in Europe.[5]

There were points of conflict that in the past could have developed into important clashes between the two countries. In 1996 U.S. Ambassador Guerra Mondragón, commenting on the previous ban on sophisticated arms sales by the United States, noted that the military was not clearly subordinate to the civilian government in Chile. He referred to the constitutional provisions that precluded the president from removing a military commander. This must have caused some concern among the military and the Frei administration, for the Chilean government immediately replied that the constitution had set up an institutional mechanism for selecting military commanders. Privately, some government officials acknowledged that they agreed with the statement but that it was unacceptable that a representative of another government would make such a declaration.[6]

In 1997 U.S. foreign policy toward Argentina provoked a minor protest from both Chile and Brazil. The United States decided to reward Argentina for its generally pro-U.S. foreign policy and especially for its participation in international peacekeeping missions, by naming it a "non-NATO ally." It may also have served to assuage Argentine concerns over the potential sale of advanced fighter aircraft to Chile.[7] The designation had little real significance in the security context of South America in the late 1990s. The new status is largely symbolic, permitting Argentina to purchase surplus U.S. weapons but not guaranteeing U.S. military protection.[8]

Before the announcement, the Chilean government expressed its concerns about the potential impact of such a designation on regional security arrangements, hoping to convince the United States to reward Argentina by some other means.[9] When asked about the issue by Foreign Minister Jose Miguel Insulza during a Bilateral Consultation Mechanism meeting, Secretary of State Albright downplayed its significance and noted that the United States was considering offering the status to other countries as well.[10] Nevertheless, Chile consulted with both Brazil and Great Britain (the British were concerned because of the Falklands/Malvinas Islands dispute) concerning the implications of Argentina's potential status.[11]

The Foreign Ministry received a barrage of domestic criticism over the possibility that a neighboring country might become a military ally of a great power. Senator Sergio Bitar, president of one of the parties of the Concertación alliance, called for a meeting of the OAS to discuss the regional security implications of such an alliance.[12] In hearings before the Defense and Foreign Relations commissions of the Chamber of Deputies, Foreign Minister Insulza declared that there were no real security disadvantages, although such extracontinental alliances did make regional integration more difficult.[13] The head of the Foreign Relations Commission, Gabriel Valdés, noted that he did not understand why the United States would choose to make such a distinction when in the past it had maintained a policy of equal treatment on security matters for all countries in the region.[14] Other voices would go further, accusing the United States of attempting to break up the new relationship among the ABC countries (Argentina, Brazil, and Chile) either because it represents a diplomatic challenge to the United States or because the United States profits by selling war material to rivals.[15]

In subsequent press interviews, Foreign Minister Insulza also expressed his puzzlement over U.S. policy.[16] Chile's Ambassador to Washington John Biehl downplayed the designation's significance. Nevertheless, he noted that: "the type of alliance and the type of peace that will develop in the post–Cold War era will be something that Latin America will have to discuss jointly, and the United States has no reason to make special alliances with one or another country, breaking the equilibrium in which we Latin Americans have been handling ourselves very well."[17]

The Clinton administration appears to have been caught by surprise at the regional reaction to its offer to Argentina. The U.S. response was ad hoc and served only to fuel irritation. First, the United States tried to get Argentina to accept an alternative designation as "Ally for Peace," but the Argentines rejected it.[18] Secretary of State Albright subsequently offered Chile the opportunity to be designated likewise, but Chile rejected it on the grounds that: "Having that category is not free. One has to be willing to send troops to Bosnia or the Gulf War, and that does not fit with our policies."[19] And finally, President Clinton sent a personal letter to President Frei suggesting that the decision to lift the arms ban on sophisticated weapons to Chile was equivalent to Argentina's designation. Frei was apparently irritated enough by the comparison to consider responding with his own letter, but cooler heads in the administration warned that a major diplomatic crisis might be developing. Foreign Minister Insulza traveled to Washington to express Chile's displeasure and indicate that Chile wished to move beyond the controversy.[20]

Another minor irritant developed over United States actions in Yugoslavia. In multilateral forums, Chile and the United States have largely seen eye to eye. As noted in Chapter One, Chilean interests in international peace, confidence-building measures in the hemisphere, and the defense of democracy coincide well with U.S. perceptions on the region's security needs. But when NATO decided to bomb Yugoslavia in 1999 during the Kosovo crisis, Chile (and most of the rest of Latin America) voiced its dissent. Sovereignty is taken very seriously in Chile, and the specter of the United States and NATO undertaking the use of force without UN leadership was especially troubling.

Human Rights Issues

Human rights issues continued to arise in the bilateral relationship, largely because Chile's domestic politics had not been able to resolve these issues internally. With the Kennedy amendment issue closed, the United States stepped gingerly around the issue of human rights in its dealings with Chile. The Clinton administration was not reticent to recognize that problems existed, as when the U.S. Immigration and Naturalization Service (INS) granted political asylum to a Chilean journalist, Alejandra Matus, who wrote a book critical of the Chilean judicial system. The Chilean Supreme Court had ordered her arrested for violating the State Security Law and had confiscated the book.[21]

General Pinochet's arrest in London, accused by the Spanish government of violating the UN's convention against torture, demonstrated how far the United States was willing to go in pursuit of better relations with Chile and to support the democratic government in Chile. The Concertación is a coalition of the major political forces that opposed General Pinochet's military government, and the United States strongly supported the creation of international war crimes tribunals to prosecute Serb politicians and military officers for atrocities in Bosnia and Kosovo. But the Concertación accepted the military's amnesty as one of the prices to pay for a transition to democracy. That domestic bargain could be upset, with unforeseen but dangerous consequences for Chile's democracy. As a result, the United States took a neutral position on whether Britain should extradite Pinochet to Spain. As Secretary of State Albright declared: "I think we believe that in Chile, the citizens of a democratic state are wrestling with a very difficult problem of how to balance the need for justice with the requirements of reconciliation. I think significant respect should be given to their conclusions.[22]

The British denied the extradition petitions of Spain and other countries against Pinochet on the grounds that he was neither physically nor mentally fit to stand trial. Upon his return to Chile, however, the Concertación and Chilean human rights NGOs found ways to pursue a legal case against the general even within the terms of the amnesty. As of this writing (February 2001) Pinochet stands accused of being the intellectual author of a series of executions of dissidents shortly after the coup. Since these people remain among the "disappeared," their bodies have never been recovered. Under Chilean law, the fact that the bodies are missing constitutes an ongoing crime of kidnapping. Consequently, the military's amnesty, which covers events until its passage in 1978, does not cover these cases. Pinochet was even stripped of his legislative immunity by the Santiago Court of Appeals in June 2000. (The Postscript discusses events in the case early in the Lagos administration.)

The U.S. government is becoming more active in the Pinochet case now that it is proceeding in Chilean courts. As noted in Chapter One, the Clinton administration has sought information on the Letelier case as well as others concerning U.S.

citizens. The Lagos administration has demonstrated a willingness to aid the investigations to the extent possible.

Economic Relations

The U.S. and Chilean economies boomed during all but the last year of the Frei administration, when Chile suffered its worst recession since 1982. As their agricultural exports boomed, the two countries found that they had mutual interests in cooperating at the World Trade Organization (WTO) to fight agricultural export subsidies in Europe.[23] That mutual economic growth also facilitated an increase in bilateral trade and investment flows from the United States to Chile. Inevitably, along with the growth in trade came efforts by producers and labor negatively affected to halt or slow down the pace. Some of these were minor irritants, such as those affected by animal and plant sanitation regulations, and the Chilean government was not averse to warning producers not to see protectionist conspiracies everywhere.[24] The United States had its own irritants concerning Chilean protectionism in pharmaceuticals, luxury autos, and whisky.[25]

But major issues were on the agenda, including the still-unresolved poisoned grapes case and an accusation of dumping against salmon exports, as well as a free-trade agreement to be negotiated. A test for the new Chile-U.S. relationship would be whether these controversies could be handled without damaging the overall relationship.

Poisoned Grapes, Part II

When Frei took office, the Federal Court of Appeals in Philadelphia was considering whether the suit filed by Chilean growers and exporters asking for damages from the U.S. government could proceed. The case was on hold until the court rendered its decision, but Chilean growers continued to prepare for their day in court.[26]

The issue gained new notoriety in December 1994, when lawyers for the grape growers used the Freedom of Information Act to uncover State Department documents pertaining to the case. Included in the documents was a transcript of a telephone call received by the U.S. embassy in Chile. The embassy operator identified the caller as the person who three months earlier had alerted the embassy about the poisoned grapes. This time the caller said that the earlier call had been a hoax against the military government. If true, Chilean claims that the grapes could not have been poisoned in Chile would be strengthened. But even if not true, this evidence had been withheld from Chilean growers and congressional committees investigating the case, as well as the U.S. courts.[27]

Chile's Congress responded quickly. It reactivated the commission in the Chamber of Deputies that investigated the case prior to its filing with the Philadelphia court. The commission held hearings and summoned the three individuals who had held the post of foreign minister during the controversy. In addition, Congress asked the government to reactivate the bilateral commission that had investigated the facts of the case during the previous year. Congress also called on the government to pursue the case further in the U.S. courts, if necessary, as well as consider activating the Bryan-Suárez Mújica treaty. Clearly, the Frei administration was under considerable domestic pressure to pursue some kind of settlement.

In January 1995 the Federal Appeals Court ruled that the Chilean case could not proceed. To the chagrin of Chile, U.S. Ambassador Guerra-Mondragón announced that the grapes case was now closed. Foreign Minister Insulza immediately replied that there were still some steps that could be taken to gain a settlement, and the Chamber of Deputies commission announced that members would travel to the United States to lobby their counterparts for some type of settlement.

The Frei administration feared that the grapes case might affect negotiations on a free-trade agreement. Foreign Minister Insulza tried to keep the two matters separate. The vice president of the Chamber, however, declared that a free-trade treaty should be negotiated with safeguards to prevent this type of action from occurring in the first place and providing for appropriate remedies if it did.[28]

In October 1995, after the U.S. Supreme Court refused to hear an appeal of the Philadelphia court's decision, Foreign Minister Insulza created a three-member commission with a representative of the exporters, to advise him on the next step. The Chamber of Deputies' Commission suggested invoking the Bryan-Suárez Mújica treaty, but Insulza apparently did not want to fan the flames by raising an option that the United States had previously rejected. The Frei administration preferred that a bilateral technical commission develop an indirect way to compensate Chilean exporters.[29]

In light of these events, Ambassador Guerra-Mondragón recognized that the case had not been closed. In January 1996, one year after his inappropriate remarks, he announced that a forthcoming visit to Chile by Secretary of State Warren Christopher could produce a mutual accord on the grapes case.[30] Within a week, Chile reopened the diplomatic path and asked the United States to reconvene the bilateral technical commission that had previously worked on the grapes case.[31]

But the Clinton administration was not cooperative. The U.S. ambassador to the OAS once again announced in February that the case was closed, provoking Insulza's rebuke that the United States could not unilaterally close the case. Assistant Secretary of State for Latin America Jeffrey Davidow, in a visit to Chile in August, made a slight modification in the U.S. position. Responding to a reporter's question, he declared that the United States would neither indemnify nor compensate Chileans in the grapes case. Chilean growers and exporters and the Chamber of Deputies Commission rejected this position. Foreign Minister Insulza, however, noted that the case would stay open until some type of satisfactory settlement were developed. He was quick to point out, however, that the case had not strained bilateral relations.[32]

In September 1996 the United States finally made an effort to gain Chilean agreement to end this irritant in the bilateral relationship. Ambassador Guerra-Mondragón announced the U.S.-proposed settlement. The United States would not pay any indemnity or direct monetary compensation, but it would offer the growers three benefits. The U.S. government would provide growers and exporters with up-to-date market prices and volumes, as well as meteorological satellite information to make Chilean marketing decisions more efficient. Ten to twenty scholarships for studying disciplines related to fruiticulture would also be provided, as would aid in facilitating imports of Chilean fruit into the U.S. market. But the president of Federación de Fruta rejected the proposal, commenting that: "We consider this offer an affront to the honor, dignity and principles of those of us who have been affected by a possible administrative error that cost Chile more than U.S. $300 million." Shortly thereafter, the growers announced that they would not accept even an arbitral award if it did not provide compensation adequate to the damages sustained by Chile.[33]

The growers and their allies continued to press the Frei administration on the issue. But the government resisted escalating the dispute in the face of U.S. reticence to consider monetary damages. In February 1997, Foreign Minister Insulza commented that President Frei would not deal with grapes or any other irritant on the bilateral agenda when he met with President Clinton later that year. The relevant technical and diplomatic groups, he said, would discuss such matters, while the president focused on the general relationship and its place in Chilean foreign policy.[34]

The Foreign Ministry did not forget about grapes: Chile proposed the creation of a high-level bilateral commission with public- and private-sector representatives to deal with agricultural questions in general, and grapes were discussed in 1999. Grape growers now held out for public U.S. recognition that they were not at fault for the alleged poisoning. The government pursued an indirect form of compensation via mechanisms that would decrease the cost of importing grapes into the United States.[35]

Salmon Dumping

Chile began salmon farming in the late 1970s with the support of the U.S. Peace Corps and the U.S. Agency for International Development. Its growth was stimulated partly by a successful U.S. antidumping case against Norwegian salmon imports. Salmon are not native to southern Chile, but entrepreneurs imported eggs from Norway, and production skyrocketed as the country became the second largest exporter in the world after Norway. Southern Chile has some inherent advantages, with clean water that is just cold enough to allow a salmon to mature four to six months earlier than in the United States and Norway. Feed prices are also cheaper, since northern Chile is a major producer of fish meal. The waters lack the diseases that attack salmon in northern waters. Producers are both Chilean and foreign enterprises (including Norwegian) and very astute: they now ship higher-value-added boneless fillets rather than the whole fish. Chilean salmon exports are concentrated in the United States and Japan. Chile accounts for 40 percent of all U.S. salmon sales and supplies Japan with 60 percent of the salmon and trout consumed in sushi.[36]

In 1996 U.S. salmon producers in the states of Maine and Washington, facing another low-cost competitor, filed a suit with the International Trade Commission (ITC) alleging that Chilean exports were both subsidized and dumped in the U.S. market. The Coalition for Fair Atlantic Salmon Trade (FAST) hired the law firm that had won the earlier victory against Norwegian salmon to represent their interests in this case. The eight firms had 440 employees and argued that they might be forced out of business if Chile were not stopped from abusing U.S. trade legislation.[37]

U.S. producers ran into a powerful transnational alliance (TNA) between Chilean producers and U.S. transporters, importers, retailers, and restauranteurs. Atlas Air Inc. hired retired Senator Robert Dole's lobbying firm, and the National Restaurant Association lobbied Congress on behalf of cheap salmon. Chilean producers hired a U.S. public relations firm that worked with U.S. restaurants and supermarket chains in an education campaign targeting consumers. The Chileans also hired a prestigious Washington, D.C., law firm, Arnold and Porter, to present their case before the ITC. The TNA claimed that if the U.S. imposed tariffs on Chilean salmon, more than 19,500 jobs in the United States would be at risk.[38]

U.S. producers gained an initial victory in July 1995, when the ITC found that there was sufficient evidence to proceed with a full-scale investigation. The ITC also accepted their claim that fillets (largely Chilean exports) and whole salmon (mainly of U.S. production) were not distinct products with different markets.[39] But the U.S. producers lost the subsidy case in November 1997 when the Commerce Department found that Chilean subsidies amounted to 0.62 percent, which is below the level requiring punitive action.[40]

In January 1998, the Commerce Department issued its preliminary findings. Dumping charges against three of the five Chilean companies were thrown out on the grounds that the dumping of less than 2 percent of fair market price did not merit the imposition of duties. Two other firms were found to be liable to duties of 3.3 percent and 8.3 percent, while imports from companies other than these five were assessed duties of 5.79 percent.[41] Duties were decreased slightly in the summer of 1998 when Chilean producers convinced the Commerce Department that an error was committed in determining the real exchange rate used in the investigations.[42] The case ended with these modest duties imposed.[43]

Chilean producers and government perceived this case as a threat to the country's entire development strategy. As Minister of the Economy Alvaro García noted: ". . . the salmon case is a particularly symbolic case, in the sense that a developing country has developed a product that has achieved great international success. . . ."[44] The antidumping legislation has been explicitly rejected by most other countries,[45] and Chile gained support for its case from countries confronting similar U.S. threats.[46]

Chile began its defense by threatening to take the issue of antidumping legislation to the WTO. The United States was confident that the WTO could not overturn this U.S. domestic legislation. Ambassador Guerra-Mondragón warned Chile that it faced a long and costly process doomed to failure. Chile persisted, and bilateral consultations within the WTO framework began in September 1997. These were preliminary discussions to determine whether an agreement could be worked out before filing a formal complaint.[47] Given the U.S. position on its antidumping legislation, these talks were indeed doomed to failure. In August 1999 Chile began consultations at the WTO concerning the feasibility of presenting a formal case.[48]

Although salmon exports were not affected by the small tariffs imposed by the United States, producers petitioned the Commerce Department in late 1999 to undertake a new study. Chilean producers believed that, based on the knowledge they had gained in how the Commerce Department calculated costs, they could now demonstrate that dumping was not occurring.[49]

The salmon case had a major impact on Chile's foreign economy policy. NAFTA's dispute resolution procedures made it difficult for the United States to apply dumping sanctions to Mexico and Canada. President Frei interpreted the case as confirmation that joining NAFTA had real trade benefits.[50] But as it became clearer that Chile was not going to become a member of NAFTA in the foreseeable future (see discussion below), the Frei administration reluctantly decided to address items on the bilateral agenda on a case-by-case basis. Juan Gabriel Valdés, Director General of International Economic Relations at the Foreign Ministry (and soon to become foreign minister himself) noted: "It appears better to us to 'grab the bull by the horns' in a moment of crisis such as we face. We are going to put the issues on the table and see where we can go."[51]

The NAFTA Fiasco

As discussed in the last chapter, the Bush and Clinton administrations had been promising Chile that negotiations on a free-trade agreement would soon begin. The NAFTA case began auspiciously for the Frei administration. Shortly after assuming office, Frei received a letter from Clinton noting his intent to make Chile the first new member of NAFTA as a result of its excellent efforts on the economy. Frei quickly sought to build on this U.S. interest by proposing the creation of a high-level consultative mechanism to examine NAFTA as well as other issues on the agenda.[52]

During the Summit of the Americas meeting in December 1994, the Clinton administration made a big show of publicly promising Chile that the process to incorporate it into NAFTA would begin. Formal discussions began in the summer of 1995. To the chagrin of U.S. negotiators but not the Mexicans or Canadians, Chile was reticent to become involved in serious negotiations until the U.S. Congress had approved the fast track.[53]

There was an initial debate within Chile concerning the merits of joining NAFTA. The largest labor organization (Central Unitaria de Trabajadores), the Mapuche indigenous people, and environmentalists all initially opposed free trade for fear that it would bring more foreign capital to exploit Chilean labor and natural resources.[54] But the labor unions quickly realized that free trade was a reality and decided to focus on affecting the terms under which it would be implemented.[55] Within the Sociedad Nacional de Agricultura (SNA), wheat and sugar producers worried about the implications of free trade, but the most dynamic sectors of agriculture were already exporting and looking anxiously at greater possibilities.[56] In short, because Chile's economy was already quite open, domestically oriented farmers, environmentalists, and indigenous peoples did not carry enough weight in Congress or the Frei administration to significantly affect Chile's commitment to free trade.

Within the United States the benefits from free trade with Chile are small and dispersed, while the pain is potentially great and concentrated. Few exporters in the United States benefit from trade with Chile: in 1994 total exports were valued at less than $3 billion. The small size of the Chilean market (13 million consumers) is not enough to convince potential exporters to use their scarce lobbying capital on Chile. In contrast, a number of U.S. industries, especially in agri- and aquaculture, face severe competition from Chile. These firms and their labor are organized and extremely active in Congress and the Commerce Department. In addition, the environmental lobby has a strong interest in reproducing its success with the NAFTA side agreements on environment in every trade agreement into which the United States enters.[57]

The U.S. political forces favoring a free-trade agreement with Chile thus needed to have a strong executive on their side. But because Clinton is a member of the Democratic Party, he had to provide some benefits to the labor and environmental groups that form an important segment of the party's constituency. A Democratic-controlled Congress passed NAFTA only because it included side agreements requiring Mexico to adhere to U.S. labor and environmental standards. For the Chilean case, House Minority Leader Richard Gephardt announced that "The NAFTA model must be the floor for any future negotiations" rather than the ceiling.[58]

The labor and environmental side agreements to NAFTA were not a concern for the Chilean government, which believed that the country's practices in these two arenas were close enough to U.S. standards so as not to become a major issue. The assistant director for public policy of the AFL-CIO, Thea Lee, also saw these issues as nonproblematic for Chile. But, Lee argued, an agreement with Chile would set a precedent for future agreements and consequently the overall agreement had to include the side agreements.[59]

Republicans favored free trade but did not want a number of the components that were included in the Mexican accession to NAFTA negotiations when the Democrats controlled Congress. Rep. Philip Crane, head of the Trade Subcommittee of the House Ways and Means Committee, stipulated that committee members would not accept side agreements.[60] As Congressional negotiations with the Clinton administration stalled, Republicans put a window dressing on their position: they would not accept side agreements that were not directly related to trade.[61] In the Senate, Majority Leader Robert Dole led a group of nine senators demanding that the NAFTA dispute process concerning dumping and export subsidies not be part of any agreement with Chile.[62]

The debate between Democrats and Republicans over the terms of free trade was suddenly complicated by the Mexican peso collapse and U.S. bailout in early 1995. Suddenly all Latin American economies became suspect, even for Republicans. In addition, by the end of 1995 Pat Buchanan had used protectionist sentiment to challenge Robert Dole for the Republican presidential nomination. Dole responded by arguing for time to "digest" the results of NAFTA and the Uruguay Round trade liberalizations before proceeding further. And finally, the wave of freshmen Republican congressmen swept in as the Congress changed hands in 1994 were isolationists unlikely to vote for new international commitments at a time when they were running for reelection in 1996.[63]

Since Chile is a minor trade partner for the United States and the world, Republicans have seen little need to compromise on their position for the sake of incorporating Chile into NAFTA. Chile's claim that the Free Trade Agreement of the Americas project has lost credibility in Latin America while the bilateral agreement with Chile has stalled, has not impressed the Republicans. The Republicans reject Clinton's version of a FTAA. Clinton may believe Chile's warnings, but his first priority is maintaining the Democratic Party's electoral coalition.

Despite the political complications of 1995 and 1996 for the Republicans, NAFTA foundered after 1996 because of the fundamental disagreement with a Democratic president over the side agreements. The Frei administration ultimately tired of being what the *Washington Post* called "America's jilted sweetheart." But since a free-trade agreement with the United States always constituted only a part of the Concertación's foreign economic policy, the damage in the area of trade has not been great. Chile entered a free-trade agreement with Mexico in 1992 and signed another with Canada in 1996 outside the NAFTA framework. Chile began enjoying some of the benefits of NAFTA itself, as U.S. companies such as Chrysler and IBM began to export to Chile from plants located in Canada and Mexico and thus subject to the lower tariffs provided by these free-trade agreements. José Joaquin Brunner, President Frei's chief of staff (secretario general), stated: "We don't need an accord with the United States anymore. Yes, we still want one, but we have made strides in other directions that have helped our economy and will continue to without a U.S. trade agreement."[64]

As for the U.S. market, Chile benefits from the Generalized System of Preferences (GSP) even without a free-trade agreement. In the first half of 1999, exports to the United States grew at triple the rate of those to Canada and twice that of those to Mexico, with whom Chile has free-trade agreements.[65] In addition to the salmon boom, perishable fruit demonstrates the possibilities of lucrative exports. Exports to the United States, which jumped from $26 million in 1996 to $40 million in 1997, prompted one berry grower and exporter to say, "How we would be favored by NAFTA, I cannot really see."[66]

Conclusion: The Key to Cooperative Relations despite Important Disagreements

And so we come to the millennium. If we looked at specific cases in isolation, it would appear that Chilean-U.S. relations are characterized by conflict and distrust, largely fueled by internal politics. But the relationship is actually quite strong, and a level of cooperation has been reached that is unique in the relationship. To understand how the specific can be contentious while the overall is cooperative, we can take another look at two cases: poisoned grapes and the NAFTA discussions.

The grape growers and exporters were not part of the Concertación constituency; rather, they were supporters of the right. But their influence, as major producers of foreign exchange and employers, was great as evidenced by the Chamber of Deputies' continued demand for a resolution that would compensate the growers. Unlike the Senate, the Chamber was dominated by the Concertación parties. Some deputies saw this less as a case of defending growers and exporters than as a test of whether the relationship would be balanced. Chile had cooperated in areas desired by the United States, even accepting international arbitration in the Letelier case. Now the deputies expected to see evidence that the United States treated Chile as an equal and would adjust its policies to accommodate issues on which Chileans felt strongly.

The Frei administration, however, had a longer view in mind. It did not want to test the relationship on what it considered a side issue. For the administration the fundamental issue was securing and promoting Chile's place in the international trading and financial political economy. Consequently, a free-trade treaty of some type with the United States was more important than the grapes issue. And the administration recognized that the U.S. Congress could make or break that agreement, so it did not want to antagonize either the Congress or the Clinton administration by pushing too hard on grapes.

The Frei administration certainly wanted NAFTA or a bilateral agreement. But failing to consummate a treaty did not leave Chile in the lurch. The mere fact that the Clinton administration desired a treaty helped Chile with other potential economic partners. U.S. interest enhanced Chilean credibility as a desirable economic partner and therefore helped Chile get the resources necessary to promote a broader-based export-led development model. The payoffs for the strategy were bilateral free-trade agreements with Canada and Mexico, as well as Mercosur's willingness to accept Chile as an associate member without abiding by its common external tariff.

Chile and the United States thus reach the millennium with a new relationship that is characterized by the greatest degree of cooperation in their history. Cooperation is not a matter of agreement on specific bilateral issues. Here there continue to be misunderstandings and irritants on important issues of the moment. Cooperation instead is the result of the United States setting a context and Chile working within it.

The United States has successfully developed an international political economy that corresponds to its view of the world and in which the United States is the hegemonic judge of who is behaving appropriately. Because the United States does not see its position at risk, as was the case during the competitive days of the nineteenth century and Cold War, even when Chile disagrees the U.S. government does not pursue efforts to undermine their Chilean counterpart. In particular, when U.S. domestic politics produce outcomes detrimental to Chile, the U.S. government does not foreclose cooperation on other matters.

Chile's first two administrations since redemocratization have understood this reality of U.S. primacy as well as the inability of Chile to contest it successfully. Rather than take the Argentine view that this new reality in the post–Cold War period means that one must constantly agree with the United States in foreign policy, the Aylwin and Frei administrations have attempted to demonstrate that following the rules still allows for respectful disagreement on particulars. Disagreement can be arrived at and dealt with in a transparent and confidence-building fashion that ultimately demonstrates to the international community that Chile is a worthwhile and credible partner.

POSTSCRIPT

SEVEN

CHILE LOOKS TO THE FUTURE WITH RICARDO LAGOS

AFTER A NARROW VICTORY OVER THE CENTER-RIGHT CANDIDATE, Ricardo Lagos assumed the presidency in March 2000 to begin his six-year term. A member of the Socialist Party, one of the founders of the Party for Democracy, and, during the military government, investigated for suspicion of attempting to assassinate Pinochet, Lagos received his doctorate in economics from Duke University in the United States. The third consecutive president of the Concertación alliance, Lagos came into office with an ambitious but not radical domestic and international agenda designed to promote economic growth with distribution and to conclude the transition to democracy by reforming the Constitution to rid it of its "authoritarian enclaves."

This book went to press after only seven months of the Lagos administration, which provided time to evaluate his priorities and initial efforts but not to gauge his possibilities for success and how this will affect Chile's relations with the United States. Consequently, in this postscript we lay out some general outlines and speculate on how the bilateral relationship may develop in light of a decade of movement toward political and economic accommodation.

The postscript has three sections. First we evaluate the domestic context in which the Lagos administration develops and identifies its program. The context is largely outside the control of the Lagos administration but has a fundamental influence on what will form part of the government's domestic agenda as well as the obstacles it confronts in implementing it. We then examine Lagos's general foreign policy agenda in order to understand how Chile's relations with the United States fit into the country's larger picture. The concluding section analyzes the many ups and few downs of the bilateral relationship during the first half-year of the Lagos presidency.

Domestic Context

Lagos assumed office with an ambitious program to reform the Constitution and remove the remaining authoritarian enclaves, modify voting requirements, and generally increase the distribution of the benefits of growth to a wider sector of Chilean society.

Among the important domestic factors with which he will have to contend is the fact that the center-right made a strong political showing in the elections, both in the presidential runoff of January 2000 and in the major mayoral races in the summer.[1] So although the Concertación gained a one-seat majority in the Senate[2] and Lagos's standing in the polls was strong, the resurgence of the center-right will undoubtedly affect Lagos's ability to implement his programs. The center-right recognizes the demand for constitutional reform and is willing to consider even eliminating the designated and lifetime Senate offices, but will demand major concessions on other matters.[3]

The legislative situation particularly affected Lagos's efforts to significantly reduce press censorship laws and reform the labor code.[4] Making use of presidential powers, Lagos did pardon a journalist convicted of violating the state security laws.[5] But there is little flexibility in what the Lagos administration can do in the area of labor reform. The national labor organization, CUT, has denounced the proposed reform for its emphasis on creating a flexible labor market and has called on the president to decide whether he is for business or labor.[6]

Despite the legislative constraints on his programs, Lagos has maintained popular support in his first half-year in office. His handling of a scandal involving severance pay for upper-echelon state employees in the Frei administration helped produce an approval rating for his administration in early October of over 60 percent.[7]

One advantage for Lagos is the recovery of the Chilean economy from its 1999 recession. While gross domestic product fell by 1.1 percent that year, it was expected to grow by around 7 percent in 2000. Unfortunately, unemployment was slow to decline from its double-digit levels, and by the end of summer and through the fall, a number of major strikes erupted. Some within the Lagos administration even advocated taking a hard line with the strikers, with the Interior Ministry threatening to mobilize Carabineros police and perhaps the Pinochet-era State Security Law against striking truckers who had blocked highways.[8]

Significant events in the area of human rights suggest that Lagos is gaining support for his programs from some unexpected places. A few weeks before Lagos took office, the British returned Pinochet to Chile, having denied the Spanish extradition request on grounds of the general's poor health. Upon Pinochet's return to Chile, the judge looking into his responsibility for human rights violations was inundated with requests for the general to be charged in specific cases. By November the number of charges officially filed against Pinochet stood at over two hundred. In the summer, the Chilean Supreme Court voted to strip the general and lifetime senator of his legislative immunity and to allow him to stand trial. In November the Supreme Court ordered that tests be conducted on both his physical and mental health.[9] He was indicted in February 2001.

At the same time that Pinochet was confronting major challenges to his ability to avoid human rights accusations, the military's unity in hiding the past and denying responsibility began to deteriorate. The Human Rights Roundtable, initiated in the final year of the Frei administration, came to an end in July 2000 with the military agreeing that unresolved questions concerning the "disappeared" persisted. The military also supported legislation providing strict anonymity for people, even military personnel, who come forward with information about the location of individuals who were "disappeared." Many opponents of the military regime protested the agreement because it provides for only an initial six-month process, renewable once by the president, and they fear that cases will be closed forever afterward.[10]

The military supported these investigations to focus on the new issues on their agenda, and the Lagos administration made it clear that modernization will proceed better once the issues of the past are resolved.[11] In addition, the top army leadership that had served under the direct command of General Pinochet is now moving into retirement, replaced by generals who have other matters of priority, as well as master's degrees and doctorates in history and political science from Chilean and foreign universities.[12] For the first time, the army attended the annual memorial service honoring former army commander in chief General Carlos Prats, Pinochet's immediate predecessor before the 1973 coup who was subsequently assassinated in Argentina. Pinochet himself, as well as his secret police, DINA, is under investigation by Argentine authorities for the murder.[13]

The shift in army sentiment was reflected in the institution's official history, which barely mentioned the military government and included only one picture of General Pinochet. Defense Minister Mario Fernandez was prompted to praise the army officially for the first time since the transition to democracy, declaring: "Well, I want to speak out and make a gesture, to go beyond all our differences. I want to be part of the homage that all of Chile gives to its army this month, this month that remembers the army's past glories."[14] In light of the fact that Septembers past also include the 1973 coup, this declaration by a member of Lagos's cabinet suggests that civil-military relations are well on their way to a significant change.

Some military officers began to break the code of silence, even publicly. In 1978 former DINA secret police operations director Pedro Espinoza, in a sworn but secret affidavit, accused Pinochet of having given the order to assassinate Letelier. Nothing came of it, and Espinoza was sentenced for the crime. But in March 2000, Espinoza repeated his charge to a newspaper reporter. Other officers began to step forward and accuse their superiors of giving orders that violated human rights. Among the most powerful was the declaration by a retired army officer who served as a guard at the National Stadium in the immediate aftermath of the coup, when thousands of opponents were imprisoned in the stadium for months and hundreds executed. In October 2000, retired air force commander in chief Fernando Matthei, a member of the junta during the 1988 plebiscite, declared on the *Medianoche* television news and interview program that Pinochet had wanted to call out the troops rather than accept the results of the vote.[15] While the information regarding the plebiscite had already been revealed in scholarly work, the fact that a member of the junta would reveal it publicly at this time was very dramatic. Brigadier General Oscar Izurieta Ferrer, cousin of army commander in chief General Ricardo Izurieta and his possible replacement in 2001, declared in September that individuals could and should ask for pardon, although "the army as an institution does not need to ask for pardon. . . ."[16]

General Foreign Relations

The guidelines for Lagos's foreign policy are respect for international law and treaties, the peaceful resolution of conflict, the defense and consolidation of democracy, respect for human rights, and the promotion of a more equitable international economic order. The administration intends to support these goals by playing an active role individually and in concert with other nations, in particular Argentina, Brazil, and the United States.

The diplomatic offensive accelerated with a trip to Argentina in May. Speaking before a joint session of the Congress, Lagos invited Argentina to help Chile create a new cultural and economic world order that would help southern cone democracies confront the challenges produced by globalization.[17] In early June, Lagos attended the "Progressive Governance for the XXI Century" conference hosted by German Chancellor Gerhard Schroeder in Berlin. Fourteen leaders, including the presidents of Argentina, Brazil, and Chile, met to discuss ways in which the globalized economy might better serve both developed and developing countries. In particular they focused on how governments might assist this process without undermining the economy.[18] Chile cosponsored the Democratic Communities Summit in Poland in June. In September, Lagos gave a speech at the United Nation's World Summit in New York City. The Chilean president called for small nations to be given a role in the decision-making process that was producing the global village. He declared that: ". . . globalization will not have a human face if we do not work to establish rules and institutions capable of guiding it in all its aspects."[19]

The Lagos administration has also sought to increase Chilean participation in international peacekeeping as a way of contributing to an international context conducive to increasing economic interactions among a greater number of states. Chile was host to the workshop "Andes 2000," in which the armies of eleven countries met to exchange professional experiences in promoting multinational and regional cooperation.[20]

The Lagos administration improved relations with Great Britain and Spain, despite the right's continued anger over the role of these countries in the Pinochet extradition attempt.[21] The human rights issue, however, continues to pressure Chile's foreign policy as Italy, Argentina, and possibly Brazil and Uruguay seek the extradition of Chileans, including General Pinochet, for trial in a variety of deaths.[22] In addition, law suits for damages suffered as a result of the military government's violations of human rights are now being filed by hundreds of exiles and foreigners against the Chilean state.[23] If successful, Lagos's budget will have to pay for the compensation. The Lagos administration was consistent in its human rights stance as it voted against Cuba in a UN vote, although it asked everyone to recognize the impact of the U.S. economic blockade.[24]

Lagos made Mercosur one of the cornerstones of his foreign policy agenda. His perception of Mercosur is more encompassing than its present organization as a customs union. For Lagos, tariff issues are secondary. In a meeting of the economic pact's presidents, Lagos expounded upon his view of a cultural, political, and social pact. The goal of this pact would be to increase its members' negotiating strength with the United States and Europe. Lagos recognized, however, that the tariff issue was a major obstacle because Chile could not raise its tariffs to the level of those existing in Mercosur, even in the expectation that they would subsequently all be lowered. Alluding to the experience under the military government, Lagos emphasized that Chile had already paid dramatic costs in lowering its tariffs once before. Mercosur's common external tariff ranges from 10 percent to 30 percent, while Chile's tariffs are currently 9 percent and programmed to fall to 6 percent by 2003. Chile's full membership in Mercosur will thus depend heavily upon the pact's ability to lower the level of its common external tariff or its willingness to admit a country and exempt it from the tariff agreement. In addition, Lagos also declared that when Chile became a full member it would push to formalize the dispute settlement mechanisms within the pact.[25]

The Instituto Libertad, founded by Pinochet and the right, opposed joining Mercosur because it claimed the part would diminish the country's autonomy and negotiating ability, not contribute to the national economy, and negatively affect trade relations with the United States and European Union (EU). The institute's leadership charged that Lagos was seeking partisan political benefits from membership with Mercosur, a charge rejected by the administration.[26]

Negotiations with the EU for a trade and investment treaty progressed as well. The EU has apparently been concerned that Chile may increase its tariff levels to those of Mercosur, but the Lagos administration has insisted that it will retain tariff autonomy when it does gain full membership in the trade pact, and consequently the EU can negotiate in complete confidence with Chile.[27] Spain, which is the second-largest foreign investor in Chile after the United States and a member of the EU, appears to be anxious to help the negotiations forward.[28]

Relations with the United States

The human rights issues, domestic and international, that had not been resolved in the past, dominated relations with the United States. A number of major new events occurred that could significantly affect the relationship in positive and negative ways. Goodwill certainly exists on both sides, but particular national interests can still clash at times.

In the area of human rights, the U.S. government added to the pressure for prosecuting these cases beyond its interest in pursuing the intellectual authors of the Letelier assassinations. The Chilean Supreme Court ruled shortly after Lagos took office on a petition from the Washington, D.C. federal court for the interrogation of forty-two Chileans associated with the military regime in connection with the Letelier assassinations. The Chilean court unanimously accepted the request, but ruled that U.S. investigators could not carry out or be present for the interrogations.[29]

Thirty-six U.S. congressmen sent President Clinton a letter requesting that the administration seek the extradition of General Pinochet to the United States to stand trial in the Letelier case.[30] U.S. Ambassador O'Leary responded to Chilean press questions that no one was excluded from the criminal investigations and that a U.S. grand jury would decide whether the Justice Department should request the extradition of a suspect.[31] Even after Pinochet's congressional immunity was lifted in Chile, U.S. Attorney General Janet Reno declared that the U.S. investigations would continue unaffected,[32] raising the possibility that Pinochet might still be a target of the U.S. justice system regardless of what Chilean justice ultimately decides for the general.

A major Chilean newspaper editorialized against U.S. requests for investigations, arguing that the broad list of those to be interrogated included many individuals who had no ties to the crime and questioning the timing of the request now that General Pinochet had returned from London. The newspaper also reported that some members of the Chilean government held these same views.[33]

The Church Committee of the U.S. Congress had held hearings after the 1973 coup on U.S. participation in destabilizing the Allende government. In 1999, the House and Senate Intelligence and Appropriations committees requested that the CIA prepare a report: "describing all of the activities of officials, secret agents and functionaries of all kinds in the intelligence community with regards to the following aspects of the Republic of Chile: (1) the assassination of President Salvador Allende in September 1973; (2) the rise of General Augusto Pinochet to the presidency of the Republic of Chile; and (3) human rights violations committed by officials or agents of former President Pinochet." Although the CIA attempted to keep many documents secret, the Clinton administration, prompted by the nongovernmental organization "National Security Archives," insisted on a thorough review. The declassified version, known as the Hinchey Report, was finally released in September 2000. The report indicates that the CIA provided money for "humanitarian reasons" to the group that assassinated army commander in chief General René Schneider in 1973, and worked with known violators of human rights during 1974 to 1977.[34]

The declassified material contained a major surprise. The CIA officially confirmed that it collected information from Chilean intelligence sources. The agency also revealed that there had been efforts to recruit the director of the Chilean intelligence services, DINA, General Manuel Contreras, and that one payment had actually been made.

This close relationship between Chilean and U.S. intelligence sources stimulated an interesting debate about whether these contacts subverted Chilean sovereignty. This was a particularly damning accusation against a military government that emphasized its nationalism and subsequently denounced U.S. meddling in Chilean affairs. There has even been speculation that the army was repulsed sufficiently by these revelations that it contributed to its distancing itself from Pinochet.[35] Consequently, these U.S. revelations may make it easier for the Lagos administration to get military support for a more professional and less politicized structure to civil-military relations.

But not all the implications of the CIA revelations were positive for the Lagos administration. The Hinchey Report indicates that the CIA provided financial support to Allende's opponents, including the Christian Democratic Party (CD) and the newspaper *El Mercurio*. Since the CD constitutes a major partner of the Concertación and *El Mercurio* is the most important daily, the Lagos administration was pressured to ask for clarification of these accusations in particular.[36]

Jorge Schauson, member of another Concertación partner, the PPD, suggested that victims of DINA could sue the U.S. government because Contreras was either an agent or informant of the CIA. The Communist Party intends to file a lawsuit in U.S. federal court against the U.S. government for its intervention in Chile during 1970 to 1973.[37] A barrage of Chilean lawsuits against the U.S. government could conceivably produce a backlash against Chile in the Republican-controlled U.S. Congress.

From his prison cell, where he is serving a seven year sentence for participating in the Letelier assassination, General Contreras admitted that he had met numerous times with CIA agents as part of the general Cold War struggle and to train DINA agents. He denied, however, having accepted money and charged that the CIA was attempting to implicate him in crimes that the CIA itself had committed. Contreras was interviewed by the FBI, which is carrying out its investigation of the Letelier murders, and claims that he provided the FBI with hundreds of documents demonstrating CIA responsibility in that assassination as well as the deaths of other regime opponents. In addition, Contreras accuses the CIA of suggesting that DINA bribe U.S. congressmen to get more favorable treatment for Chile.[38] It will be interesting to discover whether the CIA was referring to hiring lobbyists to court congressmen, which was simply perceived by Chileans as bribery. Any attempt by the CIA to promote foreign lobbying of Congress, however, will surely produce a scandal in the U.S.

On another human rights matter, the U.S. requested permission to carry out investigations in Chile concerning the disappearance of U.S. citizens Charles Horman and Frank Teruggi during the military government. The Chilean Foreign Ministry indicated that Chilean authorities would investigate any new evidence the United States might turn over to them.[39]

There were positive acts and stalemates in the area of drug control and enforcement. Although many South American countries have misgivings about the policy that the U.S. government adopted in 2000 to help the Colombian government fight narcotics traffickers in guerrilla-controlled areas, Chile supported it. Lagos himself noted that drug trafficking was a danger to everyone and thus it was important for every country to become involved in the fight against drugs.[40]

In a March 2000 visit to Chile, U.S. Attorney General Reno raised the need to modify the extradition treaty between the two countries. The treaty dates from 1900, and U.S. officials believe it is ill suited for dealing with modern criminals, especially those involved in drug trafficking. The United States has been so frustrated with the inability to extradite people from Chile that in a drug bust during the summer, officials clandestinely provided information to an alleged ringleader that Chilean authorities were about to seize him. The hope was to capture Manual Losada when he fled Chile, but instead the United States simply upset Chilean authorities when they discovered the maneuver. In retaliation for U.S. violations of the limits on its agents' activities in Chile, the Lagos administration suspended plans to open a DEA office in the northern city of Iquique. Chile continues to insist that Chilean law takes precedence for crimes committed in Chile or if the criminal is arrested in Chile.[41]

The bilateral relationship promises to become more active on the economic front, even as Lagos develops stronger trade ties with Mercosur and the EU. In June, Foreign Minister Soledad Alvear traveled to the United States to discuss, among other matters, Chile's continued interest in a bilateral trade treaty.[42]

The Clinton administration indicated that it still hoped for a trade agreement with Chile. The two major candidates for president, Vice President Albert Gore and George W. Bush, both declared that Chile was a logical candidate for a free-trade agreement, although they disagreed about the conditions under which that could occur.[43]

In pursuit of Chile's national project for sustained growth and distribution, Ricardo Lagos, socialist, will travel to Washington, D.C., in early 2001 to renew talks with U.S. President George W. Bush, Republican, about Chile's inclusion in the North American Free Trade Agreement.

NOTES

CHAPTER ONE

1. Heraldo Muñoz and Carlos Portales, *Una amistad esquiva: Las relaciones de Estados Unidos y Chile*. Santiago: Pehuén, 1987; William F. Sater, *Chile and the United States: Empires in Conflict*. Atlanta: University of Georgia Press, 1990, pp. 20–23, quote cited by Sater as February 13, 1856.
2. Emilio Meneses Ciuffardi, *El factor naval en las relaciones entre Chile y los Estados Unidos (1881–1951)*. Santiago: Hachette, 1989, pp. 29–44.
3. Sater, *Chile and the United States*, pp. 51–53; Meneses Ciuffardi, *El factor naval*, pp. 46–47; *Army and Navy Journal*, August 1, 1885, as quoted by Meneses Ciuffardi and Sater.
4. Meneses Ciuffardi, *El factor naval*, pp. 47–51; Sater, *Chile and the United States*, pp. 51–53.
5. Joyce S. Goldberg, *The Baltimore Affair*. Lincoln: University of Nebraska Press, 1986; Robert N. Burr, *By Reason or Force: Chile and the Balance of Power in South America*. Berkeley: University of California Press, 1965, pp. 194–197; Meneses Ciuffardi, *El factor naval*, pp. 53–84; Mario Barros Van Buheran, *Historia diplomática de Chile*. Santiago: Editorial Andrés Bello, 1970, p. 528.
6. Joseph S. Tulchin, *Argentina and the United States: A Conflicted Relationship*. Boston: Twayne, 1990, pp. 46–47; Arthur P. Whitaker, *The United States and the Southern Cone: Argentina, Chile and Uruguay*. Cambridge: Harvard University Press, 1976, pp. 368–372; Sater, *Chile and the United States*, pp. 89–91, 94–104; Pike, *The United States and the Andean Republics*, p. 237; St. John, *The Foreign Policy of Peru*, pp. 160–64; Frederick B. Pike, *The Modern History of Peru*. New York: Praeger, 1967, p. 232; Daniel M. Masterson, *Militarism and Politics in Latin America: Peru from Sánchez Cerro to Sendero Luminoso*, Westport, CT: Greenwood Press, 1991, p. 33. Sater notes that Britain did not make the trade when it discovered that doing so would violate the Washington Naval Armament Limitation Treaty of 1922, but he is silent on Japanese reasoning.
7. J. Lloyd Mecham, *The United States and Inter-American Security 1889–1960*, 2nd ed. Austin: University of Texas Press, 1962, pp. 122–148, 181–185, 225.
8. Michael J. Francis, *The Limits of Hegemony: United States Relations with Argentina and Chile during World War II*. Notre Dame: University of Notre Dame Press, 1977, pp. 27–36; Sater, *Chile and the United States*, pp. 105–106, 113.
9. Francis, *The Limits of Hegemony*, pp. 83–89; 93–105.
10. Francis, *The Limits of Hegemony*, pp. 39, 84–88; Sater, *Chile and the United States*, pp. 114–118.

11. Sater, *Chile and the United States*, pp. 119–132; Mecham, *The United States and Inter-American Security*, pp. 352–388.
12. O. Carlos Stoetzer, *The Organization of American States*, 2nd ed. Westport, CT: Praeger, 1993, pp. 48–52; Muñoz and Portales, *Una amistad esquiva*, pp. 56–61; James Petras, *Politics and Social Forces in Chilean Development*. Berkeley, CA: University of California Press, 1969, pp. 104–113.
13. Paul E. Sigmund, *The Overthrow of Allende and the Politics of Chile, 1964–1976*. Pittsburgh: University of Pittsburgh Press, 1977, pp. 34–35.
14. Christián Gazmuri, Patricia Arancibia, and Alvaro Góngora, *Eduardo Frei Montalva (1911–1982)*. Santiago: Fondo Cultura Económica, 1996.
15. Joaquín Fermandois, "Chile y la cuestión cubana 1959–1964." *Estudios Históricos*, No. 5. Instituto de Historia, Universidad Católica de Chile.
16. Gazmuri, Arancibia, and Góngora, *Eduardo Frei Montalva*.
17. Sigmund, *The Overthrow of Allende and the Politics of Chile*, pp. 77–110.
18. Sigmund, *The Overthrow of Allende and the Politics of Chile*, pp. 112–118.
19. Sigmund, *The Overthrow of Allende and the Politics of Chile*, pp. 118–120.
20. Joaquín Fermandois, *Chile y el mundo 1970–1973. La Política exterior del gobierno de la Unidad Popular y el sistema internacional*. Santiago: Universidad Católica, 1985.
21. Leopoldo Gonzáles, et al., *Teoría y praxis internacional del gobierno de Allende*. México: Centro de Relaciones Internacionales, Facultad de Ciencias Políticas y Sociales, UNAM, 1974.
22. González, et al., *Teoría y praxis*.
23. Theodore Moran, *Multinational Corporations and the Politics of Dependence*. Princeton: Princeton University Press, 1974, pp. 212–215; Joaquín Fernandois, *Chile y el mundo 1970–1973*.
24. Paul E. Sigmund, *The United States and Democracy in Chile*. Baltimore: Johns Hopkins University Press, 1993, pp. 48–78.
25. Facultad Latinamericano de Ciencias Sociales(FLACSO), Santiago, Chile. Calculations from U.S. Department of State, World Bank, and IADB publications.
26. Sater, *Chile and the United States*, p. 190.
27. Heraldo Muñoz and Carlos Portales, *Una Amistad Esquiva*.
28. Sigmund, *The United States and Democracy in Chile*, pp. 87–107.
29. Augusto Varas, *Los militares en el poder*. Santiago: Pehuén, 1987, pp. 150–175; Muñoz and Portales, *Una amistad esquiva*, pp. 89–161; Sigmund, *The United States and Democracy in Chile*, pp. 111–117.
30. Heraldo Muñoz, *Las relaciones exteriores del gobierno militar chileno*. Santiago: Editorial Ornitorrinco, 1986.
31. *Qué Pasa?* (Santiago) December 6–12, 1979, pp. 8 & ff.
32. Cf. Muñoz, *Las relaciones exteriores del gobierno militar chileno*.
33. Cf. Jorge Castañeda, *Utopia Unarmed*. New York: Knopf, distributed by Random House, 1993.
34. Carlos Portales, "Estados Unidos y transición a la democracia en Chile: 1985–1986," in *Estados Unidos y Chile hacia 1987*, Edgardo Boeninger et al., Santiago: FLACSO-Chile, 1987, p. 20.
35. Boeninger, op. cit. p. 27.
36. Carlos Portales, "Estados Unidos y la transición a la democracia"; Sigmund, *The United States and Democracy in Chile*, pp. 141–178.
37. House of Representatives of the United States of America. "Restablishment of Democracy in Chile." Material for consultation only. US Embassy in Chile, August 11, 1989.

38. *El Mercurio*, July 16, 1988.
39. *El Mercurio*, October 6, 1988, and October 7, 1988.
40. Sigmund, *The United States and Democracy in Chile*, pp. 181–183.
41. Rhoda Rabkin, "The Aylwin Government and 'Tutelary' Democracy: A Concept in Search of a Case," in *Journal of Interamerican Studies and World Affairs*, 34:4 Winter 1992–1993, pp. 119–194.
42. Sigmund, *The United States and Democracy in Chile*, p. 186.
43. Ministerio de Relaciones Exteriores de Chile, Oficina de Promoción de Exportaciones, *ProChile*, 1997.
44. Comité de Inversiones Extranjeras, Chile.
45. Sebastian Edwards, *Crisis and Reform in Latin America: From Despair to Hope*. Oxford: Oxford University Press, 1995, pp. 75–76.
46. Stephen D. Krasner, "Are Bureaucracies Important: (Or Allison Wonderland)," *Foreign Policy*, 7 summer 1972, pp. 159–179.
47. Speech by Chile's President Frei at Joint Session of U.S.Congress, February 27, 1997. FLACSO Archives.
48. Speech by President Clinton before the National Congress of Chile Valparaíso, April 17, 1998. Published by the Information and Cultural Service of the U.S. Embassy. Official text. 1998. Translation by the authors.
49. Remarks by President Eduardo Frei Ruiz-Tagle. Dinner in honor of President of United States of America, Santiago, April 16, 1998, Palacio de La Moneda.
50. Bill Clinton, Speech at Inaugural Session, Summit of the Americas II. April 18, 1998. Translation by the authors from text by Instituto Chileno Norteamericano.
51. Arthur P. Whitaker, *The Western Hemisphere Ideal*. Ithaca, NY: Cornell University Press, 1954.
52. Francisco Rojas Aravena, "Chile: cambino político e inserción internacional 1964–1997, presented at the seminar "From Frei to Frei," Stanford University, April 1997.
53. Thomas Cardamone, "Arms Sales to Latin America." *Foreign Policy in Focus* 2:53, December 1997, as cited in "Latin American Civil-Military Security," latamcml @american.edu, December 16, 1997.
54. Cf. Brian Loveman, "Mision Cumplida? Civil-Military Relations and the Chilean Political Transition." *Journal of Interamerican Studies and World Affairs*, 33:3, Fall 1991, pp. 35–74; and "Protected Democracies and the Military Guardianship: Political Transitions in Latin America. 1978–1993." *Journal of Interamerican Studies and World Affairs*, Vol. 32, No. 2, Summer 1994, pp. 105–189.
55. For the Chilean case, cf. Sigmund, *The United States and Democracy in Chile*, pp. 48–56.
56. Cf. Jeanne Kirkpatrick, *Dictatorships and Double Standards*. New York: American Enterprise Institute, 1982.

CHAPTER TWO

1. Kenneth Oye, *Cooperation under Anarchy*. Princeton, NJ: Princeton University Press, 1984; Robert O. Keohane, *After Hegemony*. Princeton, NJ: Princeton University Press, 1986.
2. Neorealist theory argues that in a bipolar world these small states cannot affect the relative balance between the two great powers (Walt, *Theory of International Politics*. New York: Random House, 1979). But policy-makers in the United States and the USSR believed the competition to be global and showered governments and rebels in small states around the world with a wide variety of aid.

3. Cf. I. William Zartman and Victor A. Kremenyuk, eds., *Cooperative Security: Reducing Third World Wars*. Syracuse, NY: Syracuse University Press, 1995; Edward A. Kolodziej and Roger E. Kanet, eds., *Coping with Conflict after the Cold War*. Baltimore: Johns Hopkins University Press, 1996.
4. Barry B. Hughes, *Continuity and Change in World Politics: Competing Perspectives*, 4th ed. Upper Saddle River, NJ: Prentice Hall, 2000, pp. 210, 212.
5. The United States is the only democratic country in which a minor can be given a death sentence. Amnesty International, *United States of America: "A macabre assembly line of death." Death Penalty Developments in 1997*. April 1998, AMR 51/20/98, p. 14.
6. William R. Evinger, ed., *Directory U.S. Military Bases Worldwide*, 3rd. ed. Phoenix, AZ: Oryx Press, 1998.
7. Carlos Portales, "Seguridad regional en Sudamérica: escenarios prospectivos," in Augusto Varas, ed., *Paz, desarme y desarrollo en América Latina*. Buenos Aires: Grupo Editor Latinoamericano, 1987, pp. 333–382; Olga Pellicer, ed., *Regional Mechanisms and International Security in Latin America*. Tokyo: United Nations University Press, 1998.
8. "Clearing Army Border Mines Will Take 11 Years: Ottawa Convention Prompts Revelation that 250,000 Mines Lie on Frontiers." *Santiago Times*, November 26, 1999.
9. "Chile and Peru Sign Historic Port Access Accord: Implementation of 1883 Peace Treaty Heralded." *Santiago Times*, November 15, 1999.
10. David R. Mares, "Strategic Balance and Confidence Building Measures in Latin America: The Historical Utility of an Ambiguous Concept," in Joseph S. Tulchin and Francisco Rojas Aravena, eds., *Strategic Balance and Confidence Building Measures in the Americas*. Palo Alto, CA: Woodrow Wilson Center Press and Stanford University Press, 1998, pp. 139–157.
11. Under a constitutional amendment adopted in 1958 and modified by the military government in 1976, a portion of the state revenues generated by copper exports is to be used for equipment for the armed forces. Francisco Rojas, ed., *Gasto militar en América Latina*. Santiago: CINDE and FLACSO-Chile, 1994, pp. 255–256. In 2000, newly elected President Ricardo Lagos expressed his desire to repeal these special provisions.
12. Venezuela purchased F-16s in the early 1980s, but without the sophisticated radar the Chileans are seeking.
13. Ministry of National Defense, *Libro de la defensa nacional*, 1997; Chapter 1; Arturo Fuenzalida Prado, "Chile y las operaciones de mantenimiento de la paz." *Revista de Marina*, No. 6, 1999, pp. 549–558.
14. Soledad Alvear, inaugural statement, international seminar on peacekeeping, Santiago, May 15, 2000.
15. The official declaration can be found at www.minrel.cl, March, 25, 1999. Translation by the authors.
16. John Gerard Ruggie, "International Regimes, Transactions and Change: Embedded Liberalism in the Postwar Economic Order." *International Organization*, Spring 1982, 36:2; David R. Mares, *Penetrating the International Market*. New York: Columbia University Press, 1987, pp. 3–28.
17. Benjamin Cohen in collaboration with Fabio Basagni, *Banks and the Balance of Payments: Private Lending in the International Adjustment Process*. Montclair, NJ: Allanheld, Osmun & Co., 1981.
18. Cohen, *Banks and the Balance of Payments*, pp. 11–29.
19. In 1999 Ecuador ceased payments on its debt, sparking fears that others might con-

front similar problems. Nicholas Moss, "U.S. & Canada: Ecuador to Meet Creditors." *Financial Times*, June 7, 2000, p. 7.

20. In 1999 Brazil tried to stem the outflow of capital by devaluing, but by the middle of 2000 analysts were expecting another devaluation. "Nervousness Increases Demand for Hedge." *Gazeta Mercantil Online* (São Paulo), May 23, 2000.
21. Javier del Rio, "La integración económica latinoamericana y caribeña en la década de los noventa." *America Latina Hoy* (Spain), 1997, pp. 5–10; Hector Vega, "Problemas de la integración Latinoamericana." *Temas regionales* (Chile), No. 1, 1998, pp. 1–13; Alfredo Guerra-Borges, "La integración centroamericana en el umbral del siglo. Una evaluación económica y política." *Revista Nueva Sociedad*, 162, July/August 1999, pp. 136–151; Marion Bywater, *Andean Integration: A New Lease on Life?* London: The Economist Intelligence Unit, 1990; Riordan Roett, ed., *Mercosur: Regional Integration, World Markets*. Boulder: Lynne Rienner, 1999.
22. Gert Rosenthal, "Un enfoque crítico a 30 años de integración en América Latina." *Nueva Sociedad*, 113, May-June 1991, pp. 60–65.
23. See Robert A. Pastor, *Congress and the Politics of U.S. Foreign Economic Policy, 1929–1976*. Berkeley, CA: University of California Press, 1980; Gilbert R. Winham, *International Trade and the Tokyo Round Negotiation*. Princeton, NJ: Princeton University Press, 1986, pp. 3–14.
24. Robert Devlin, "El plan Brady: ha surgido finalmente una solución al problema de la deuda?" *Cono Sur*, Vol. VIII, No. 3, pp. 1–2; John Williamson, "The Progress of Policy Reform in Latin America," in John Williamson, ed., *Latin American Adjustment: How Much Has Happened?* Washington, DC: Institute for Economics, 1990, pp. 414–418.
25. John Williamson, "What Washington Means by Policy Reform," in Williamson, ed., *Latin American Adjustment*, pp. 7–20.
26. George Bush, Speech on the new relationships in the hemisphere, Washington, DC, June 27, 1990.
27. Claudio Fuentes and Carlos Martin, *La nueva agenda argentino-chilena*. Nueva Serie FLACSO, Santiago: FLACSO-Chile, 1998.
28. Chile joined APEC in 1994 and it signed the Mercosur and EU treaties during 1996.
29. An introduction to the historical-sociological strain is found in Seven Steinmo, Kathleen Thelen, and Frank Longstreth, eds., *Structuring Politics: Historical Institutionalism in Comparative Analysis*. New York: Cambridge University Press, 1992; for the public choice view, see Douglass C. North, *Institutions, Institutional Change and Economic Performance*. New York: Cambridge University Press, 1992.
30. Regimes are types of international institutions consisting of rules, norms, principles, and decision-making procedures. For a discussion of regimes in international politics, see Robert O. Keohane, *After Hegemony: Cooperation and Discord in the World Political Economy*. Princeton, NJ: Princeton University Press, 1984.
31. Francisco Rojas, *Globalización, América Latina y la diplomacia de cumbres*. Santiago: FLACSO-Chile, 1998, pp. 201–232.
32. The inter-American community did not take any concrete actions to punish or coerce Fujimori into annulling the controversial May 28, 2000, elections and holding fair elections. He fled to Japan largely due to a domestic scandal that began when his intelligence chief was caught bribing a congressman.
33. Ministerio de Defensa Nacional de Chile, *Libro de la Defensa Nacional de Chile*. Santiago: Imprenta de la Armada, 1998.
34. Fernando Bustamante "La cuestión de las medidas de confianza mutua en el contexto de sub-región andina," in Francisco Rojas Aravena, Ed., *Balance estratégico y medidas*

de confianza mutua. Santiago: FLACSO-Chile, 1996, pp. 195–216; Adrían Bonilla, ed. *Ecuador-Peru: horizontes de la negociación e el conflicto*. Quito: FLACSO-Ecuador, 1999; General Barbosa de Figueiredo (Brazilian Army and participant in MOMEP), "¡Una misión cumplida!" *Military Review* (Ecuador), September-October 1999, pp. 76–80.

35. Jason Blair, *New York Times*, reprinted as "Precedente del caso Pinochet." *El Mercurio*, Santiago, May 6, 2000, p. 2.
36. Text of the letter published in *Diario La Segunda*, Santiago, March 28, 2000. Translation by the authors.
37. Letter cited in www.elmostrador.cl, May 31, 2000. Translation by the authors.
38. *El Mercurio*, June 22, 2000, p. C-2.
39. Ethan A. Nadelmann, "Global Prohibition Regimes: The Evolution of Norms in International Society." *International Organization*, 44:4, Autumn 1990, pp. 479–526.
40. Paz Milet, "La lucha contra el narcotraficante desde la perspectiva Chilena," in Paz Milet, ed., *Narcotráfico y serguridad en América Latina*, Santigao: FLACSO-Chile, 1997.

CHAPTER THREE

1. Kenneth N. Waltz, *Theory of International Politics*. New York: Random House, 1979, pp. 122–123.
2. Timothy R. Scully, "Reconstituting Party Politics in Chile," in Scott Mainwaring and Timothy R. Scully, eds., *Building Democratic Institutions: Party Systems in Latin America*. Stanford, CA: Stanford University Press, 1995, p. 125.
3. Scully, "Reconstituting Party Politics in Chile," p. 125.
4. *Constitution Chilean 1980*, official text revised by Fernando Silva Sanchez, Viña del Mar, March 1993, p. 60; Chapter 11, Articles 95 and 96.
5. *Constitution Chilean 1980*.
6. Claudio Fuentes, "The Military and Politics: Weaknesses in Chilean Democracy." Paper presented at the Annual Convention of the Latin American Studies Convention, Chicago, 1998.
7. Delia M. Boylan, "Taxation and Transition: The Politics of the 1990 Chilean Tax Reform." *Latin American Research Review*, Vol. 31, No. 1, 1996. *Chilean Constitution 1980*, Chapter 12, Articles 97 and 98.
8. *Chilean Constitution 1980*, Chapter 4, Article 32, no. 10.
9. *Chilean Constitution 1980*, Chapter 4, Article 25.
10. *Chilean Constitution 1980*, Chapter 4, Article 32, no. 17 and 21.
11. Samuel Kernell and Gary C. Jacobson, *The Logic of American Politics*. Washington, DC: Congressional Quarterly Press, 2000, p. 369.
12. Karl W. Deutsch, Jorge I. Domínguez, and Hugh Heclo, *Comparative Government: Politics of Industrialized and Developing Nations*. Boston: Houghton Mifflin, 1981, pp. 77–80; Kernell and Jacobson, *The Logic of American Politics*, p. 235.
13. National Public Radio coverage, November 7, 2000. The Democratic Party, expecting the majority of these urban voters to choose the Democratic candidate, went to court to get the polls to stay open late, but the Republicans were able to convince a higher court to rule that polling places had to close on time despite the fact that citizens would be unable to exercise their right to vote.
14. For Reagan's victory, *Statistical Abstract of the U.S., 1999. Twentieth-Century Statistical Trends*, 1999, Table 1445; for voter turnout, Deutsch, Domínguez, and Heclo, *Comparative Government*, p. 30.
15. Kernell and Jacobson, *The Logic of American Politics*, pp. 167–169.

16. Editorial, "GOP Sounds a Sour Note; Clinton's Attack: President Loses Test-Ban Treaty Vote but Gains by Attacking Republicans' Negativism." *Baltimore Sun*, October 22, 1999, p. 22A.
17. Jack W. Germond and Jules Witcover, "Voters Tuning in to Campaign Reform." *Baltimore Sun*, April 5, 2000, p. 11A; Foster, "Election Reform Dies Aborning." *Milwaukee Journal Sentinel*, June 19, 2000, p. 08A.
18. Peter B. Evans, Harold K. Jacobson, and Robert D. Putnam, eds., *Double Edged Diplomacy: International Bargaining and Domestic Politics*. Berkeley, CA: University of California Press, 1993.
19. Raymond Tatalovich and Byron W. Daynes, *Presidential Power in the United States*. Monterey, CA: Brooks/Cole, 1984, p. 263.
20. Tatalovich and Daynes, *Presidential Power*, p. 267.
21. Lawrence Freedman, *U.S. Intelligence and the Soviet Strategic Threat*, 2nd ed. Princeton, NJ: Princeton University Press, 1986, pp. 8–29.
22. Frederick H. Hartmann and Robert L. Wendzel, *To Preserve the Republic*. New York: Macmillan, 1985, pp. 141–143.
23. Douglas Johnson and Steven Metz, "Civil-Military Relations in the United States: The State of the Debate." *The Washington Quarterly*, 18:1, 1994, pp. 197–213.
24. Since 1993, factionalization within the RN has become more apparent. Andrés Allamand, the party president, is a leader with liberal tendencies, whereas the more conservative sector includes a group of senators who, during 1995, explicitly rejected agreements reached by the political commission working on the reform of the Constitution.
25. See the 1989 and 1993 platforms of the Concertación for a further elaboration of these principles.
26. Eduardo Aninat, "Chile en los noventa. Las oportunidades del desarrollo." *Finanzas y Desarrollo* (IMF), March 2000.
27. See Carlos Figueroa, "Una diplomacia para el desarrollo." Paper prepared for the Ministry of Foreign Relations, Chamber of Deputies, April 5, 1994, and "Bases programáticas del Segundo Gobierno de la Concertación." *Un gobierno para los nuevos tiempos*, Santiago: Concertación de Partidos por la Democracia, 1993, mimeo.
28. See Francisco Rojas Aravena, *La Reinserción International de Chile*, 1991; *De la Reinserción a los Acuerdos*, 1992; *Consolidando una inserción múltiple en el sistema internacional*, 1993; and *Construyendo un nuevo perfil externo: Democracia, modernización, pluralismo*, 1994, each published by FLACSO-Chile.
29. Eduardo Frei, Presidential Speech to the National Congress, May 21, 1994; Edmundo Pérez Yoma, "Inauguración del año académico de las Fuerzas Armadas." *Fuerzas Armadas y Sociedad*, No. 2, FLACSO-Chile, 1995; and Edmundo Pérez Yoma, "Inauguración del año académico de las academias de guerra." *Fuerzas Armadas y Sociedad*, No. 1, FLACSO-Chile, 1996.
30. Pérez Yoma, "Inauguración del año académico de las academias de guerra."
31. Augusto Varas and Claudio Fuentes, *Defensa nacional, Chile 1990–1994. Modernización y desarrollo*. Santiago: FLACSO Book Series, 1994.
32. *Memorial del Ejército* [Official Records of the Army], issue dedicated to "Conquista y consolidación de las fronteras interiores: una tarea del ejército," No. 445, Santiago, 1994. For the army, the most relevant documents include Augusto Pinochet, "Ejército, trayectoria y futuro," August 21, 1992; and "Ejército de Chile: posibles elementos a considerar en su proyección futuro," August 19, 1993.
33. See discussion in Chapter One.
34. Manuel Antonio Garretón, "Coaliciones políticas y proceso de democratización: el

caso chileno," *FLACSO Documentos de Trabajo* 22, 1992, and *Hacia una nueva era política*. Santiago: Fondo de Cultura Económica, 1995, esp. chap. 5.

35. For a general overview of the human rights question during the democratic transition, see José Zalaquett, "Derechos humanos y limitaciones políticas en las transiciones democráticas del Cono Sur," *Colección de Estudios CIEPLAN* 33, 1991, pp. 147–186.
36. Garretón "Coaliciones políticas y proceso de democratización," chap. 7.
37. Claudio Fuentes, *El discurso militar en la transición Chileno: mesianismo, autonomia, y conviviencia en democracia*. Nueva Series FLACSO (1996, in press). On the army's view of its role, see *Presentación del Ejército de Chile ante la Comisión Nacional Verdad y Reconciliación*, Vol. 1, Santiago: Ejército de Chile, 1990.
38. "Army Readies System to Gather Info on Disappeared." *Santiago Times*, June 23, 2000.
39. Kernell and Jacobson, *The Logic of American Politics*, p. 416.
40. Kernell and Jacobson, *The Logic of American Politics*, p. 412.
41. The U.S. refusal to join the League of Nations and desire to remain aloof from Asian and European wars are supposed to indicate U.S. isolationism between the two world wars. Yet the United States was very active in the European financial dilemmas of the 1920s, signed a number of bilateral treaties outlawing war, and maintained troops throughout the Caribbean basin until 1933. During the 1930s the United States was active in the Pan American Union.

CHAPTER FOUR

1. Carlos Portales, Transnacionalización y Política Exterior Chilena, Documento de Trabajo FLACSO, 126, 1981.
2. Hughes, *Continuity and Change in World Politics*, pp. 185–187.
3. Cf. the discussion of transnational alliances among Mexican vegetable growers and U.S. consumer groups, senators from importing states, and U.S. businesspeople engaged in importing, distributing, and selling Mexican produce. David R. Mares, *Penetrating the International Market*. New York: Columbia University Press, 1987, pp. 203–225.
4. Dominique Hachette and Rolf Luders, *Privatization in Chile: An Economic Appraisal*. San Francisco: Institute for Contemporary Studies, 1993, pp. 59–61; 99–114.
5. An interesting historical parallel is found in Brazil's alliance with the United States to oppose Latin American efforts to prohibit the use of military force to collect debts owed to foreign nationals. Brazil was a creditor nation at the time. E. Bradford Burns, *The Unwritten Alliance*. New York: Columbia University Press, 1966, p. 121.
6. U.S. Statistics, 1999, from www.census.gov.
7. Departamento Económico Embajuola de Chile en Estados Unidos, *Trade and Investment between Chile and the United States*, Santiago: Editorial Trineo SA, 1998, p. 14.
8. Sigmund, *The United States and the Return to Democracy in Chile*, pp. 174–177.
9. Paul Shepard, "La Raza Ceremony Honors Border Deaths." *Contra Costa Times*, July 3, 2000, p. A10.
10. Mike Claffey and John Marzulli, "Self-Policing Not Finest." *Daily News* (New York) July 7, 2000, p. 6; Scott Glover and Matt Lait, "Most of Perez's Allegations Are Confirmed, Panel Told; Rampart: Testimony in Another Officer's Hearing Says 70–80% of Informants' Charges Have Been Corroborated." *Los Angeles Times*, June 20, 2000, p. 1; DeWayne Wickham, "Civilian Board Would Purge Corrupt Cops." *USA Today* September 9, 1996, p. 19A; www.amnestyusa.org/rightsforall/police.

11. See the publications of the Southern Poverty Law Center, *SPLC Report* and *Intelligence Report*.
12. U.S. Census, 1997, www.census.gov.
13. U.S. Statistics, 1999, Table 9, www.census.gov.
14. U.S. Census, 1997, www.census.gov.
15. Information from Fundación Ford, Santiago, 1999.
16. Cf. David Stoll, *Is Latin America Turning Protestant?: The Politics of Evangelical Growth*. Berkeley, CA: University of California Press, 1990.
17. Personal observation by David Mares, Del Mar, CA, November 5, 1999.
18. Eduardo Gallardo, "Chile Gives American Millionaire Go-Ahead for Huge Nature Preserve." Associated Press, July 8, 1997, from http://web.lexis-nexis.com/universe/document, p. 2; Hugh Davies, "US Fashion Magnate Is Demonised in Paradise." *Daily Telegraph* July 9, 1997, from http://web.lexis-nexis.com/universe/document.
19. "Tompkins Case Nearing Solution." *Santiago Times*, October 9, 1995; "Government Divided over Tompkins Case." *Santiago Times*, October 16, 1995.
20. CHIPNews, "DC Senator Says Foreign Investors Threaten National Sovereignty," December 7, 1995.
21. "Las acusaciones y sus respectivas defensas ¿Qué tienen contra Tompkins?" *La Epoca*, March 30, 1997.
22. "Un gran parque puede desarrollar las fronteras interiores." *La Tercera*, July 1, 1997. From www.latercera.cl.
23. "Debate Continues over Huinay Fundo." *Santiago Times*, December 15, 1995; "Tompkins Given Environmental Award." *Santiago Times*, January 18, 1996.
24. "U.S. Congressmen Concerned about Tompkins." *Santiago Times*, October 5, 1995.
25. "Tompkins Case Nearing Solution." *Santiago Times*, October 9, 1995.
26. "Government Divided over Tompkins Case." *Santiago Times*, October 16, 1995.
27. "Los puntos del acuerdo entre Gobierno y Douglas Tompkins." *La Tercera*, June 20, 1997. From www.latercera.cl.
28. *La Tercera*, July 8, 1997.
29. Lewis Dolinsky, "An Ecologist Gets the Shaft." *San Francisco Chronicle*, June 5, 1998, p. A14.

CHAPTER FIVE

1. Cf. Carlos Portales and Juan Gabriel Valdés, "El futuro de las relaciones Chileno-Norteamericanas," in Heraldo Muñoz, ed., *Chile: política exterior para la democracia*. Santiago: Pehuén, 1989, p. 186; *Programa de Gobierno*. Santiago: Concertación de Partidos por la Democracia, 1990, pp. 34 ff; speech of Foreign Minister Enrique Silva Cimma at the Consejo Chileno de Relaciones Exteriores, Santiago, May 8, 1991; Presidential Message, May 21, 1991.
2. *La Tercera*, January 2 and 22, 1991; *Que Pasa*, February 1989; Sigmund, *The United States and Democracy in Chile*, pp. 117–118, 128.
3. *El Mercurio*, September 25, 1991; Sigmund, *The United States and Democracy in Chile*, p. 191.
4. "EEUU planea US$ 1.1 millón en ayuda militar a Chile." *La Tercera*, March 3, 1991.
5. Marcos Robledo, "Las relaciones Chile-Estados Unidos en el ámbito militar." *Fuerzas Armadas y Sociedad*, VI:2, April/June, 1991, pp. 5–25.
6. "USAF reanuda programas de asistencia a FACh." *La Tercera*, March 13, 1991.
7. "Anuncian visita de oficiales de la Marina de EEUU." *El Mercurio*, March 19, 1991; "Confirmada adquisición de aviones de transportes para FACh." *El Mercurio*, March

20, 1991; "Ministerio de Defensa analiza compra de material bélico a EEUU." *El Mercurio,* May 7, 1991; "ENAER podrá recibir repuestos para sus aviones de combate de EEUU." *El Mercurio,* August 8, 1991; "Armada Nacional y Guardacostas de EEUU en actividades de control de narcotráfico." *El Mercurio,* July 31, 1991.

8. "Diputado Makis denuncia restricción de EEUU en ayuda militar a Chile." *La Segunda,* October 9, 1991; "Aspectos relevantes de proyecto del Senado de EEUU referente a asistencia militar a Chile." *El Mercurio,* October 10, 1991; "Clarificación de Embajada de EEUU." *El Mercurio,* October 10, 1991; "Aviso al congreso de EEUU es procedimiento normal." *El Mercurio,* October 10, 1991; "Embajada en EEUU precisa alcances de ley de ayuda militar." *El Mercurio,* October 11, 1991; "RN señala que norma de asistencia militar sería discriminatoria a Chile" and "Declaración de la Embajada de Estados Unidos." *El Mercurio,*" October 11, 1991; "RN solicita a Embajador de EEUU aclaración sobre proyecto de ayuda militar." *El Mercurio,* October 17, 1991; and "Ministros aclaran proyecto de restricción de ayuda militar de EEUU." *El Mercurio,* October 23, 1991.
9. "Cardoen demanda a aduana de EEUU." *El Mercurio,* May 24, 1991; "Gobierno no tomará parte en demanda de Carlos Cardoen en EEUU." *La Tercera,* March 10, 1992; "Parlamentarios de Oposición y Gobierno critican retención de helicóptero de Cardoen en EEUU." *La Tercera,* March 15, 1992; "Cancillería estudiará caso helicóptero de industrias Cardoen." *El Mercurio,* March 19, 1992; "Cancillería no ha recibido fallo en favor de Cardoen." *La Tercera,* October 10, 1992.
10. "Reportaje sobre Carlos Cardoen y su relación con EEUU." *El Mercurio,* May 16, 1993; "EEUU retoma indagación en torno a Carlos Cardoen." *El Mercurio,* May 18, 1993.
11. George Bush, Speech on the new relationships in the hemipheres. Washington, DC: U.S. Embassy in Chile, June 27, 1990.
12. See the declarations of RN president Andrés Allemand in *El Mercurio,* December 1, 1990.
13. Danilo Kusmanic and Pedro Sierra, *Percepciones de los actores de la minería Chilena en torno al acuerdo de libre comercio con Estados Unidos* and Jacqueline Weinstein, *Informe de síntesis a partir de las entrevistas con los agentes del sector pesquero,* Santiago: FLACSO-Chile, Proyecto de Investigación sobre Acuerdo de Libre Comercio entre Chile y Estados Unidos, December and August, 1991, respectively.
14. Alicia Frohmann, *Acuerdo de libre comercio Chile-Estados Unidos: la perspectiva del movimiento sindical,* Santiago: FLACSO-Chile, Proyecto de Investigación sobre Acuerdo de Libre Comercio entre Chile y Estados Unidos, May 1992.
15. Pilar Bascuñán, *Percepciones de las principales asociaciones empresariales sobre el acuerdo de libre comercio Chile-Estados Unidos,* Santiago: FLACSO-Chile, Proyecto de Investigación sobre Acuerdo de Libre Comercio entre Chile y Estados Unidos, September 1991; see also the survey by the American Chamber of Commerce (in Chile) published in *The Journal* (Santiago), October 1991.
16. John Maggs, "U.S. Likely to Put Off Chile Talks on Trade; Congressional Fight Worries Bush Aides." *Journal of Commerce,* May 13, 1992.
17. Andrea Butelmann and Alicia Frohmann, *Percepciones de actores oficiales y privados en Estados Unidos ante la iniciativa Bush,* Santiago: FLACSO-Chile and CIEPLAN, serie: *Relaciones Económicas Internacionales Chile/EEUU,* 1, March 1991, p. 8.
18. Alejandro Foxley, *De la reinserción a los acuerdos: La política exterior Chilena en 1991.* Santiago: FLACSO-Chile, 1992.
19. Curtis W. Kamman, "Chile y los Estados Unidos en una economía global de mercado." Official Text. Santiago: U.S. Embassy, April 3, 1992.

20. Sylvia Saborio, "Avoiding a Patchwork of FTAs." *Journal of Commerce*, May 28, 1992, p. 6A.
21. "Bush, Chilean President Meet, But Trade Talks Uncertain." *Journal of Commerce*, May 14, 1992, p. 2A.
22. Steven Greenhouse, "Trade Talks with Chile are Planned." *New York Times*, May 14, 1992, p. D1.
23. "Califican de erronea gira presidencial a los Estados Unidos." *El Mercurio*, May 18, 1992; *La Epoca*, May 18, 1992; "Senadora del PPD desalentada por anuncio sobre acuerdo de libre comercio." *El Mercurio*, May 14, 1992.
24. "Presidente de la CPC desalentado por anuncio de Estados Unidos." *El Mercurio*, May 15, 1992; "Senador de RN de acuerdo con anuncio del gobierno de Estados Unidos." *La Epoca*, May 14, 1992; "AMCHAM forma Consejo Acuerdo de Libre Comercio." *El Mercurio*, May 15, 1992.
25. "Gobierno de Estados Unidos solicitará extensión del 'Fast Track.'" *El Mercurio*, May 14, 1992; "Canciller y Secretario de Estado suscriben acuerdo de cooperación." *El Mercurio*, May 15, 1992; "Foxley destacó status de relaciones bilaterales con Estados Unidos." *La Tercera*, May 18, 1992.
26. "Comisión parlamentaria descarta envenenamiento de uva en Chile." *El Mercurio*, January 25, 1991; "Sobresedimiento judicial reafirma posición chilena ante FDA." *El Mercurio*, February 7, 1991; Sigmund, *The United States and Democracy in Chile*, pp. 181–183, claims that the U.S. and Chilean studies are inconclusive as to where the poisoning could have occurred.
27. "Gobierno dispuesto a agotar instancias para lograr compensación por caso uvas envenenadas." *El Mercurio*, August 31, 1991.
28. "EEUU no se siente responsable en caso uvas." *El Mercurio*, September 18, 1992.
29. "Cámara y Senado piden convocar Comisión Bryan." *El Mercurio*, January 6, 1993; "Gobierno recurrirá a Comisión Bryan." *La Epoca*, January 6, 1993; "Exportadores discrepan de Enrique Correa en caso uvas." *La Tercera*, January 8, 1993; "Exportadores de fruta pidieron convocar Comisión Bryan." *El Mercurio*, January 9, 1993.
30. "Exportadores de fruta en desacuerdo con decisión de Gob. en caso uvas." *El Mercurio*, March 21, 1993.
31. "Categórico rechazo de fruteros a posición de embajador en EEUU." *El Mercurio*, March 6, 1993.
32. "Chile invitó a EEUU a reunir Comisión Bryan." *El Mercurio*, March 30, 1993; "EEUU rechazó convocar comisión Bryan por caso uvas." *La Epoca*, July 30, 1993.
33. "Solicitan al gobierno cambios en la legislación farmaceútica nacional." *El Mercurio*, August 8, 1991; "Industria farmaceútica de Estados Unidos exige cambios a la ley de patentes nacional." *La Epoca*, August 3, 1992.
34. "Estados Unidos interesado en firmar otros acuerdos con Chile." *El Mercurio*, June 16, 1992; "Chile hará una sola negociación sobre acuerdo con Estados Unidos." *El Mercurio*, June 17, 1992.
35. "Clinton reiteró compromiso de ALC con Chile." *El Mercurio*, May 5, 1993.
36. Sigmund, *The United States and Democracy in Chile*, p. 168.
37. "Burocracia de EEUU impide reingreso de Chile al SGP." *El Mercurio*, January 24, 1991; "Protesta parlamentaria por no reincorporación al SGP." *El Mercurio*, January 25, 1991; "Presidente del Senado viajó a EEUU para analizar razones de demora con SGP." *El Mercurio*, January 28, 1991; "Firmando decreto de reintegro de Chile al SGP." *El Mercurio*, February 5, 1991; "Burocracia de EEUU atrasó reintegro de Chile al SGP." *La Tercera*, February 6, 1991.

38. "Armada Nacional y Guardacostas de EEUU en actividades de control de narcotráfico." *El Mercurio*, July 31, 1991.
39. "Policías chilenos serán entrenados en EEUU." *El Mercurio*, October 10, 1992; "Piden a EEUU instalar oficina del FBI en Chile." *El Mercurio*, July 17, 1993; "PPD estima negativa invitación a FBI." *El Mercurio*, July 19, 1993; "Gobierno aclara alcances de oficina del FBI en Chile." *El Mercurio*, July 20, 1993; "General Stange se refirió a personal de DEA." *El Mercurio*, July 21, 1993; "Rechazo a instalación de oficina del FBI." *El Mercurio*, July 21, 1993; "Categórico rechazo de min. Krauss a críticas por FBI." *El Mercurio*, July 22, 1993.
40. "Reportaje sobre embajador de EEUU." *La Segunda*, July 24, 1993.
41. "Fallo de Corte Suprema de Estados Unidos ni es válida en Chile." *La Tercera*, June 17, 1992; "Presidente rechaza fallo judicial norteamericano." *La Tercera*, June 18, 1992; "Decisión de Corte Suprema de Estados Unidos no afecta a convenios vigentes con Chile." *El Mercurio*, June 20, 1992; "Gobierno rechaza dictamen de la Corte Suprema de los Estados Unidos." *El Mercurio*, June 23, 1992.
42. "RN rechaza fallo de la corte suprema de los Estados Unidos." *La Tercera*, July 8, 1992.

CHAPTER SIX

1. John O'Leary, "U.S.-Chilean Bilateral Defense Relations and Regional Security: A View from Embassy Santiago." Remarks at the Academia Nacional de Estudios Políticos y Estratégicos, ANEPE, Santiago, June 7, 2000.
2. Dave Poole, "Documentary on War Games Both Terrific, Tiresome." *Columbus Dispatch*, December 7, 1997, p. 4J.
3. Calvin Sims, "U.S. Weighs Lifting Curb on Arms Sales to Latin America." *New York Times*, July 21, 1996, p. I:3.4
4. Leslie Crawford, "Latin America Lures Warplane Makers: US Plan to Lift an Arms Sales Ban Has Created a Furor." *Financial Times*, August 13, 1997, p. 4.
5. "Fach Not Interested in Second Hand Jets." *Santiago Times*, November 24, 1999; Mark Mulligan, "U.S. Seeks to Boost Arms Sales to Chile." *Financial Times*, November 17, 1999, p. 16.
6. Polémica crean opiniones del embajador de EE.UU." *El Mercurio*, July 23, 1996; "Guerra-Mondragón afinó polémicos dichos." *La Epoca*, July 24, 1996; "Roce diplomático." La Epoca, July 28, 1996; "Progresismo paradógico." *La Epoca*, August 1, 1996.
7. Sims, "U.S. Weighs Lifting Curb on Arms Sales."
8. George E. Condon, Jr., "Clinton Extends Special Status; Grants Argentina 'Non-NATO Ally' Label." *San Diego Union-Tribune*, October 17, 1997, p. A-2.
9. "Chile pedirá precisiones a los EE.UU." *El Mercurio*, August 10, 1997; "Chile expondrá inquietudes a Washington." *El Mercurio*, August 12, 1997; "Persiste duda sobre alianza EE.UU.-Argentina." *La Epoca*, August 13, 1997; "Castigo a una estrategia." *El Mercurio*, August 17, 1997.
10. "EE.UU. ofrece ampliar status de 'aliado.'" *El Mercurio*, August 14, 1997.
11. "Análisis Chile-Gran Bretaña sobre status argentino." *El Mercurio*, August 15, 1997.
12. "Relaciones con EE.UU." *El Mercurio*, August 16, 1997; "Piden reunión de la OEA para analizar caso de aliado estratégico." *El Mercurio*, August 17, 1997.
13. "Canciller Insulza expuso las implicancias del status Argentina-EE.UU." *El Mercurio*, August 21, 1997.
14. "Valdés: 'Debemos mantener la cabeza fría.'" *La Epoca*, August 24, 1997.
15. Karin Ebensperger, "Chile y Estados Unidos." *El Mercurio*, September 5, 1997. See also declarations in similar vein by ex-president of Brazil, Jose Sarney in "José Sarney: 'EE.UU. quiere desestabilizar el Mercosur.'" *La Epoca*, August 21, 1997.

16. "EE.UU. está metiendo la cola en Sudamérica." *La Tercera,* August 31, 1997.
17. "Enrevista al embajador chileno en Estados Unidos John Biehl." *El Mercurio,* October 5, 1997.
18. "Chile: 'opciones abiertas' con EE.UU." *La Nación,* September 14, 1997.
19. "Entrevista a José Miguel Insulza." *Ercilla,* May 4, 1998.
20. "La 'mini-crisis' de la carta de Clinton: entretelones." *La Segunda,* September 2, 1997.
21. "Black Book Casts Shadow Over Guadalajara Fair." *Santiago Times,* November 30, 1999.
22. Thomas W. Lippman, "U.S. Keeps Low Profile on Pinochet; Officials Don't Want Precedent Set." *Washington Post,* December 6, 1998, p. A22. This article also notes that the United States fears that if Pinochet is forced to stand trial, U.S. military officers who served in Vietnam might be arrested in some countries. Although the United States did release thousands of classified documents concerning the military's killings shortly after the coup, the British courts had ruled that Pinochet could not be charged for violations that occurred before Chile signed the UN treaty under which he is being charged.
23. "Farm Subsidies Top Agenda at WTO Meeting." *Santiago Times,* November 30, 1999.
24. "Entrevista al embajador chileno en Estados Unidos John Biehl." *El Mercurio,* October 5, 1997.
25. O'Leary was the new U.S. Ambassador. "Entrevista a John O'Leary." *La Tercera,* August 23, 1998.
26. "Chile prepara defensa para nueva instancia en caso uvas." *El Mercurio,* April 29, 1994.
27. Bruce Ingersoll, "Grape Scare of 1989 May Have Been a Hoax, Phone Transcript Indicates." *Wall Street Journal,* December 23, 1994, p. B:5A; William R. Long, "Between U.S. and Chile, A Grape Divide." *Los Angeles Times,* December 31, 1994, A:2.
28. "Gobierno rechaza vinculación entre caso de uvas y Nafta." *El Mercurio,* January 28, 1995; "Negociaciones del Nafta no pueden desvincularse de caso uvas envenenadas." *El Mercurio,* March 30, 1995.
29. "Suprema de EE.UU. desechó demanda por 'Caso Uvas.'" *El Mercurio,* October 3, 1995; "Entrevista al Canciller José Miguel Insulza." *La Segunda,* January 29, 1996.
30. "Prevén posible 'arreglo mutuo' en caso de uvas." *El Mercurio,* January 27, 1996.
31. "Chile reactivó vía diplomática para caso uvas." *El Mercurio,* February 2, 1996.
32. "EE.UU. no puede cerrar unilateralmente caso uvas." *El Mercurio,* August 21, 1996.
33. "Rechazan solución de EE.UU. en caso de uvas." *El Mercurio,* September 3, 1996.
34. "Frei excluira" temas bilaterales de agenda en su visita a EE.UU." *El Mercurio,* February 13, 1997.
35. *Financial Times.* "EE.UU. y Chile reabren caso uvas envenenadas." *La Tercera,* October 21, 1999; "Embajador de EE.UU. y el caso uvas: 'Apreciamos que se haya presentado esta propuesta.'" *La Tercera,* October 22, 1999; "Chile negocia con EE.UU. ventajas para envíos de fruta." *El Mercurio,* November 4, 1999.
36. Stewart A. Baker, "Chile's Road to Joining NAFTA." *Journal of Commerce,* May 4, 1995, p. 8A; Mark Mulligan, "Chilean Fish Farmers Fend Off Poachers, Predators, Lawyers: Salmon and Trout Producers Are Boosting Exports after Finding Out What Their Markets Want." October 27, 1999, p. II:38; "Guerra-Mondragon: 'salmoneros chilenos lograron lo mejor.'" *El Mercurio,* January 16, 1998.
37. Peter Passell, "Salmon Eaters Salute a Victory against the Protectionists." *New York Times,* January 22, 1998.
38. Passell, "Salmon Eaters Salute a Victory against the Protectionists"; Mulligan,

"Chilean Fish Farmers Fend Off Poachers, Predators, Lawyers"; Nancy Dunne, "Chile fights US over Salmon." *Financial Times*, January 13, 1998; Kevin G. Hall, "US-Chile Salmon Dispute Spawns Political, PR Wars: Farmers Have a Bone to Pick over Pricing." *Journal of Commerce*, October 24, 1997, p. 5A. Arnold and Porter formed part of the TNA that successfully defended the Mexican tomato growers in a dumping suit during the 1970s. David R. Mares, *Penetrating the International Market: Theoretical Considerations and a Mexican Case Study*. New York: Columbia University Press, 1987, pp. 203–225.

39. Kevin G. Hall, "ITC Finds Injury in Chilean Salmon Case." *Journal of Commerce*, July 25, 1997, p. 3A; Kevin G. Hall, "US Salmon Farmers Lose Round against Chile, But Keep Fighting." *Journal of Commerce*, November 14, 1997, p. 3A.
40. Hall, "US Salmon Farmers Lose Round against Chile."
41. Nancy Dunne, "US Rules on Salmon Dumping Claim." *Financial Times*, January 10, 1998, p. 4.
42. "Salmones: un triunfo." *El Mercurio*, July 17, 1998.
43. "Chile to Seek Accord with US on Salmon." *Journal of Commerce*, October 8, 1998; "Gobierno apoya presentación ante OMC." *El Mercurio*, August 13, 1998; Mulligan, "Chilean Fish Farmers Fend Off Poachers, Predators, Lawyers."
44. "Industria del salmón desmiente 'Dumping.'" *El Mercurio*, September 3, 1996; "Canciller refuta tésis de conspiración imperialista." *El Mercurio*, July 19, 1997; "Biehl: 'Si fallan contra los salmones sería pésima señal.'" *La Epoca*, January 3, 1998; quote is from "Salmoneros: comienza batalla legal decisiva." *El Mercurio*, July 3, 1997.
45. James Baxter, "WTO Doomed from Start: Negotiators." *The Gazette*, (Montreal), December 5, 1999, A6.
46. "Mercosur apoyará a Chile por conflicto del salmón." *La Epoca*, July 30, 1997.
47. "Gobierno insistió ante EE.UU. que puede recurrir a la OMC." *El Mercurio*, July 19, 1997; "Guerra-Mondragón: 'son pequeños escollos en una excelente relación,'" *La Epoca*, July 25, 1997; "Comienzan consultas bilaterales con Estados Unidos ante la OMC." *La Epoca*, September 25, 1997.
48. "Gobierno considera pedir un panel a la OMC por el caso salmones." *El Diario*, August 2, 1999.
49. "Gobierno considera pedir un panel a la OMC"; "Salmoneras piden revisar sobretasa." *El Mercurio*, August 4, 1999.
50. "Frei: ingreso de Chile al Nafta reduciría problemas con EE.UU." *La Epoca*, July 3, 1997; John Maggs, "Dispute Rule at Center of Debate over Chile; Senators Want NAFTA Provision out of Deal." *Journal of Commerce*, August 24, 1995, p. 3A.
51. "Chile cambia estrategia comercial con EE.UU." *El Mercurio*, October 7, 1998.
52. *El Mercurio*, March 3, 1994; *La Epoca*, March 27, 1994.
53. Kevin G. Hall, "US: NAFTA Negotiations Too Slow; Chile: Talks Are Learning Experience." *Journal of Commerce*, August 2, 1995, p. 8A.
54. Christina Nifong, "Nothing from NAFTA, Chilean Critics Say." *Christian Science Monitor*, December 15, 1994, p. 7; "Chile espera resultado de fast track para definir agenda con EE.UU." *La Epoca*, June 22, 1994.
55. "CUT condiciona regreso a diálogo sobre Nafta." *El Mercurio*, January 27, 1995.
56. Gabriel Escobar, "Various Lobbies Pose Tough Choices for Chile as It Prepares to Join NAFTA." *Washington Post*, December 25, 1994, p. A33.
57. Baker, "Chile's Road to Joining NAFTA"; Richard Lawrence, "Chile's Proposed NAFTA Entry Draws Mixed US Response." *Journal of Commerce*, June 20, 1995, p. 2A.
58. John M. Goshko and Peter Behr, "34 Hemispheric Leaders to Seek Free Trade Pact;

NAFTA Partners Also Planning to Issue an Invitation to Chile." *Washington Post,* December 8, 1994, p. A31.

59. Kevin G. Hall, "GOP Trade Leader: No Side Accords for Chile." *Journal of Commerce,* December 15, 1994, p. 1A; Anthony Faiola, "Chile Takes Its Trade Elsewhere: Delay of U.S. 'Fast-Track' Legislation Makes Canadian and Mexican Products More Attractive." *Washington Post,* December 25, 1997, p. A29.
60. Hall, "GOP Trade Leader."
61. John Maggs, "Agreement on Fast Track Trade Authority Proves Elusive." *Journal of Commerce,* October 17, 1995, p. 3A.
62. Maggs, "Dispute Rule at Center of Debate over Chile."
63. John Maggs, "House Crafting Bill to Save Chile Talks; Political Concerns Complicate Fast-Track Effort." *Journal of Commerce,* December 13, 1995; Nancy Dunne and Guy De Jonquieres, "Fast Track Is Going Nowhere—Administration and Congress Are Divided over US Trade Measure." *Financial Times,* October 9, 1995, p. 3.
64. Faiola, "Chile Takes Its Trade Elsewhere"; the Chilean Ambassador to the United States made similar remarks. "Arriagada: 'Un acuerdo de libre comercio con EE.UU. no es vital para Chile'." *El Diario,* May 13, 1999.
65. "NAFTA y UE, Unicas Regiones a Las que Crecen Exportaciones." *El Mercurio,* July 7, 1999.
66. Richard Read, "Chile Doing Fine Without NAFTA." *The Plain Dealer,* November 28, 1997, p. 11B.

CHAPTER SEVEN

1. "Right Surges in Municipal Elections." *Santiago Times,* October 30, 2000.
2. By virtue of a right-wing senator's suspension while under criminal investigation and Pinochet's absence from the Senate, the Concertación holds a 24 to 23 advantage. "Frei Assumes Lifetime Seat Today." *Santiago Times,* March 21, 2000.
3. "Right Agrees to Limited Constitutional Reform." *Santiago Times,* June 27, 2000.
4. "Freedom of the Press in Chile." *Santiago Times,* October 31, 2000; "Workers Criticize Diluted Labor Reforms." *Santiago Times,* November 9, 2000.
5. "Journalist Receives Presidential Pardon." *Santiago Times,* July 7, 2000.
6. "Union Leader Condemns Labor Law Reforms." *Santiago Times,* November 13, 2000.
7. "Chile: President Ricardo Lagos Wins Approval for Handling of Scandal, Truckers Strike." *NotiSur—Latin American Affairs,* ISSN 1060–4189, Vol. 10, No. 39, October 27, 2000. Since the truckers' strike did not occur until after the poll had been taken, this headline is misleading.
8. "Government Prepares for National Truckers Strike." *Santiago Times,* October 31, 2000.
9. "Chile: Gen. Augusto Pinochet Stripped of Immunity." *NotiSur,* ISSN 1060–4189, Vol. 10, No. 29, August 11, 2000.
10. "Relatives of Disappeared Removed from Congress." *Santiago Times,* June 22, 2000.
11. "Defense Chief Calls for Accord with the Past." *Santiago Times,* March 28, 2000.
12. "New Army High Command Breaks Links with Past." *Santiago Times,* November 3, 2000.
13. "Army Attends Prats Memorial for the First Time." *Santiago Times,* October 3, 2000.
14. "Official Army History Book Nearly Omits Pinochet." *Santiago Times,* September 15, 2000.
15. "Espinoza Says Pinochet Ordered Letelier Murder." *Santiago Times,* March 24, 2000; "Former Guard Confirms Stadium Murders." *Santiago Times,* June 28, 2000; "Pinochet Wanted to Call Out the Troops." *Santiago Times,* October 6, 2000; "Military

Confessions Break Code of Silence: Corbalan and Others Admit Guilt in Operation Albania." *Santiago Times*, November 7, 2000.
16. "General Calls for Repentance and Reconciliation." *Santiago Times*, September 22, 2000.
17. "Lagos Calls for New Economic Order." *Santiago Times*, May 19, 2000.
18. "Lagos Attends Conference in Berlin." *Santiago Times*, June 1, 2000; "Lagos Debuts on World Stage." *Santiago Times*, June 5, 2000; "Lagos Evaluates Berlin Conference." *Santiago Times*, June 6, 2000; "Crean foro de países ricos y emergentes." *El Mercurio*, June 5, 2000.
19. "Lagos Optimistic about Globalization Process." *Santiago Times*, September 7, 2000.
20. "Sube presencia de Chile en las fuerzas de paz." *El Mercurio*, June 27, 2000.
21. "Relations with England and Spain Eased." *Santiago Times*, October 6, 2000; "Chile and Spain Resume Diplomatic Relations." *Santiago Times*, June 23, 2000; "Prats Family Seeks Pinochet Extradition." *Santiago Times*, October 6, 2000.
22. "Court Rules on Iturriaga Extradition Appeal." *Santiago Times*, November 10, 2000; "Region: Former Military throughout Region Implicated in Operation Condor Crimes." *NotiSur*, ISSN 1060–4189, Vol. 10, No. 24, July 7, 2000.
23. "Family of Carmelo Soria Sues State." *Santiago Times*, June 27, 2000; "Exiled Chileans Seek Compensation." *Santiago Times*, October 27, 2000.
24. "Chile Votes against Cuba on Human Rights Issue." *Santiago Times*, April 19, 2000.
25. "Lagos busca asumir liderazgo en Mercosur." *El Mercurio*, July 15, 2000; "Chile Moves Closer to Full Membership in MERCOSUR." *NotiSur*, ISSN 1060–4189, Vol. 10, No. 27, July 28, 2000.
26. "Advierten sólo 'beneficio político' en Ingreso al Mercosur." *El Mercurio*, July 29, 2000.
27. "Negociación con UE Sigue Vigente." *El Mercurio*, September 22, 2000.
28. "Chile and Spain Resume Diplomatic Relations." *Santiago Times*, June 23, 2000.
29. "Autorizan interrogatorios pedidos por EE.UU." *La Tercera*, March 14, 2000; "Fiscales Norteamericanos no pueden actuar en Chile." *El Mercurio*, March 24, 2000; "United States Presses Letelier Investigation." *Santiago Times*, March 15, 2000.
30. "Diálogo Lagos-Clinton excluyó caso Pinochet." *El Mercurio*, June 4, 2000.
31. "Nadie está fuera de amplitud de la investigación." *El Mercurio*, June 30, 2000.
32. "EE.UU. seguirá investigación de caso Letelier." *El Mercurio*, August 11, 2000.
33. "Exhorto Norteamericano." *El Mercurio*, March 23, 2000.
34. "Report Links CIA and Chilean Secret Police." *Santiago Times*, September 9, 2000; Pascale Bonnefoy, "La CIA pagó a Manuel Contreras." *El Mostrador*, Santiago, September 19, 2000, from www.elmostrador.cl.
35. "Army Reportedly Preparing an About Face." *Santiago Times*, September 25, 2000.
36. "Diplomatic Note Prepared for CIA Case." *Santiago Times*, September 28, 2000; "Nota diplomática a Estados Unidos por el caso de CIA." *El Mercurio*, September 27, 2000; *La Segunda*, Santiago, September 28, 2000, p. 28.
37. "Schaulsohn: afectados por Dina-CIA podrían lograr millones de dólares en demanda a EE.UU." *La Segunda*, September 26, 2000; "Communists Prepare Lawsuit against Tio Sam." *Santiago Times*, October 3, 2000.
38. "Chile Requests Additional Information Following Release of C.I.A. Report." *NotiSur*, ISSN 1060–4189, Vol. 10, No. 35, September 29, 2000; "Encubrimiento de la CIA en el crimen de Letelier." *El Mercurio*, September 21, 2000; "The CIA Killed Letelier: US Agency Also Suggested Bribing Five U.S. Senators, Says Former DINA Secret Police Head Manuel Contreras." *Santiago Times*, September 22, 2000.
39. "Cancillería contestó a solicitud de EE.UU." *El Mercurio*, June 20, 2000; "Cancillería y

Petición de EE.UU." *El Mercurio,* June 22, 2000; "Chile Requests Additional Information."

40. "Chile Will Support Colombia Plan." *Santiago Times,* October 12, 2000.
41. "Chile and United States Review Extradition Laws." *Santiago Times,* September 12, 2000.
42. "Alvear to Meet with US Secretary of State." *Santiago Times,* May 30, 2000.
43. "Bush promete intensa unión económica con Latinoamérica." *El Mercurio,* August 26, 2000; "Chile es un candidato obvio al tratado de libre comercio." *El Mercurio,* September 21, 2000.
44. "Lagos Optimistic about Globalization Process." *Santiago Times,* September 7, 2000.

INDEX